CLASS VOICE AND THE AMERICAN ART SONG:

A Source Book and Anthology

by

HELEN LIGHTNER

THE SCARECROW PRESS, INC.
Metuchen, N.J., & London   1991

British Library Cataloguing-in-Publication data available

Library of Congress Cataloging-in-Publication Data

Lightner, Helen, 1917–
    Class voice and the American art song : a source book and anthology / [compiled]
by Helen Lightner.
        p.   cm.
    Includes bibliographical references and index.
    "The songs" (with piano acc.) : p.
    ISBN 0-8108-2381-0 (acid-free paper)
    1. Singing—Instruction and study. 2. Songs with piano. 3. Songs, English—United
States. I. Title.
MT820.L693   1991   70885
783—dc20   91-7428

To all those students of the past and present
who have been an abiding inspiration
in the writing of this book

Contents

Acknowledgments

The author is deeply indebted to Mrs. Barbara Duke, artist and teacher of singing, for the drawings in this book. To Dr. Walter Kob, retired associate professor of music at New York University, for his arrangement of "My days have been so wondrous free" by Francis Hopkinson, as well as for his careful reading of the manuscript of this book. To Dr. Gordon Myers, retired professor of music, Trenton State University, for his setting of "When Jesus Wept" by William Billings. To Mr. Eric Foster, for his invaluable help with copyright permissions. To Mrs. Ruth Hilton, music librarian, for her great help with the proofreading and indexing of this book. And, lastly, to the memory of Mr. George Fergusson, the great teacher who pointed the way.

Introduction

This *Source Book* is intended to serve three purposes, as (1) a guide to voice class procedures; (2) a rational, tested system for the development of fundamental vocal technique, adaptable to either class or private instruction; and (3) an anthology of art songs by American composers for use as primary material in the voice class. Each of the three parts of the *Source Book* is devoted to one of these purposes, as follows.

Part I. Guide to Voice Class Procedures. This provides specific recommendations concerning such matters as class size, the expected outcomes of a one-year course, the physical arrangement of the voice class, the use of the vocalises presented in Part II, class routines, assignments, practice, how to study a song, solo versus group singing of exercises and songs, etc. A lesson-by-lesson sequence of study has not been provided in the *Source Book*. Rather, the materials that explain the basic principles of vocal technique, as well as the basic exercises helpful in the development of vocal technique, have been provided for the judicious use of the instructor in the guidance of students.

Part II. On Vocal Technique. This incorporates an empirical approach to the fundamentals of voice production, including such items as posture and breathing, as well as an explanation of the necessary coordination of all physical aspects of the singing mechanism. Specific study suggestions and special exercises are provided. A complete and scientific explanation of voice production has not been included in the *Source Book,* as this was not deemed applicable to voice class instruction. References to such studies have been provided in the bibliography for consultation by interested teachers and students.

Part III. A Collection of Art Songs by American Composers. The songs are suitable as the main feature of the voice class to which the general development may relate. They have been selected from the range of the history of the American art song and embody a variety of compositional techniques and vocal styles. Biographical material has been provided in order to point out the significance of each composer and his contribution to American music. This material provides for the correlation of voice study with the appreciative and aesthetic aspects of American vocal music, past and present. Each song is accompanied by a brief discussion of its stylistic features, to encourage the development of musical awareness and to aid the student in gaining interpretive and artistic insights. The specific study suggestions relate particularly to the application of the development of vocal technique.

The ideas, procedures, and general approach presented in all three parts of the *Source Book* have been tested successfully by the author over many years, both in class and in individual instruction in her work at New York University.

HELEN LIGHTNER
New York University

Part I
Guide to Voice Class Procedures

The voice class is an important part of the curriculum of any department of music education. Every student, irrespective of performing medium, can benefit from a study of the voice and the literature for the voice. The future composer must know and understand the voice, with all its possibilities as well as its limitations, in order to write effectively for this unique instrument. The future conductor—whether of the orchestra or of the chorus—must know and understand the voice in order to attain the best possible results when working with voices. The future teacher, regardless of area of specialization, must know and understand the voice not only to teach more effectively, but also to develop the insight and discrimination to recognize and to guide potential talent.

A unique kind of experience can be given the emerging adult in the voice class. The student singer learns that he or she is not alone in his or her efforts and that most problems are not unique. One learns that everyone has a voice but each individual voice has its own special problems. It is reassuring to hear one's peers and to work out vocal problems together. The spirit of friendly competition can encourage the student to put added effort into his or her study. Furthermore, through the performance aspect of the class, young singers not only develop vocally but also can be helped and encouraged to develop poise and self-confidence.

The fundamental technique of singing can be taught efficiently in the voice class. In the early stages of vocal study the technical elements are the same for all young voices, regardless of classification. The neophyte singer must absorb a new "language" through singing with others, listening to others, and occasionally singing a solo.

In addition to learning a new "language," the act of singing is one that demands enormous physical coordination if positive results are to be attained. Such coordination or, in other words, the simultaneous functioning of all parts of the vocal mechanism for the perfection of tonal beauty, requires time for its achievement. The development of the technical elements in singing is physical in nature and, as in any athletic activity, requires a long period of routine repetition. The voice class situation is particularly beneficial for the beginning singer as it is not only more pleasurable during the early period of study but it also allows more contact hours with an instructor during a semester's time than is possible in a private lesson plan of study. The pressure for continuous singing, as in the private lesson, is eliminated. However, students have the advantage of continuous instruction through listening to their peers and to the critical commentary of the instructor. The students achieve not only a degree of technical competence themselves, but also, and perhaps more important, an appreciation of this technique as a means for greater expressiveness in the interpretation of song literature.

Another extremely positive value in the work of the voice class is the opportunity for a wider contact with song literature. In the context of the class situation it is possible to expose the student to a much greater selection of repertoire than is possible in the private lesson. Many songs of worth can be presented without thought to the perfection or performance, as no perfection is possible in the early stages of study. Rather, the interest and enthusiasm of the students can be kept alive through the singing of songs of charm that have an emotional element of some strength. If this appeal is present in the beginning stages of study there is hope that the student will desire to go on to a deeper study of the art of singing.

The songs selected for use in the first-year voice class should be in the English language, and the selection may very well include many songs by American composers. In this way, the language barrier that faces the majority of American students in voice study will be removed, and students can thus become acquainted with songs from a wide range of the history of American music, a literature often neglected in voice training. The songs should reflect and support the developmental technical work of the student at this early stage of growth and yet be attractive and singable for the young voice. Furthermore, the songs chosen may serve to introduce the student to the compositional techniques and vocal styles embodied in the American art song. The textual content of songs selected should include the widest possible variety of human experience, thus fusing intellectual and emotional meanings and allowing for maximum expressive possibilities.

By the end of the first semester of study the student should have been introduced in easy stages to the fundamentals of vocal technique as well as all of the basic exercises for the voice. Students should have a mastery of good posture for singing, an understanding of the breathing mechanism, and a developing awareness of the refinement of coordination between posture and breathing that is necessary for tonal development. Furthermore, by the end of the first semester the student should know and be able to perform a minimum of ten songs demonstrating the musical and technical learnings of the semester.

The work of the second semester should be a development as well as a consolidation based on the work of the first semester. Students should continue to develop self-confidence in their ability to perform through a deepening understanding of the vocal mechanism as well as an increasing knowledge of the repertoire.

Class Management

Should school administrative policies make it possible, class size should be limited to no more than fifteen students. The comfortable atmosphere of the small class is more conducive to confidence among the students and to the attainment of positive results. Beginning students need a supportive ambience for their first attempts in the use of a new performing medium. In the small class the students readily know one another and are supportive of one another, and self-assurance can grow.

The physical arrangement of the voice class is an important consideration. Should the class be sufficiently small, a semicircular plan, in which all students stand in one row, may be used. This plan permits the instructor to move freely among the students, attending to individual needs but without sacrificing the group action at any time. No attempt need be made to place similar voice classifications together since all voices, male and female, learn and perform together throughout each lesson. In the early stages of study, the basic technical principles of voice production are the same for all voices and may be taught most effectively and efficiently in the class situation. Each vocal exercise and every song should be performed in unison most of the time. The range and tessitura of each selection in the *Source Book* has been carefully monitored in order to make this possible.

Each lesson should be characterized by a consistency of approach. Fifteen to twenty minutes of the one-hour class period should be sufficient for vocalises and technical explanations. However, in the first two lessons it is suggested that a modicum of explanation be used in order to allow the students to gain some confidence in the use of the voice.

Following the first lessons of the semester it is advisable to adopt a moderate routinization of the class period in order to utilize limited time in the most efficient manner. Technical explanations should be concise and clearly demonstrated. As the vocalises are being sung in unison, the instructor may move from student to student, listening to each individual closely and at the same time checking the posture and breathing mechanism. Corrective explanations based on individual needs may be made between exercises for the benefit of the entire class.

Following the vocalises, new material to be assigned may be read at sight. This activity prepares the students for their practice time by insuring that they have some feeling for the song, or songs, as whole entities. Furthermore, it helps them in both melodic and rhythmic sight-reading as well as in an understanding of other musical aspects such as tempi and phrasing. Also, at this time, the text should be discussed in order that poetic meanings be clearly understood. Commentary concerning the relationship of compositional techniques to textual needs is also beneficial.

The remaining half of the period should be spent on the assigned song of the day as well as in a review of songs studied earlier in the semester. During this portion of the lesson it is advisable to utilize selected sections of a song for the direct application, or carry-over, of technical learnings to the performance of the song itself.

Supplemental Class Activities

1. Recording of Voices

At the beginning of the first semester it is a most useful activity to record, on tape, the performance of one song by each student in the class. This may be one of the songs from the *Source Book* or any song familiar to the student. At the end of the first semester of study, and again at the end of the second semester, this activity should be repeated. By means of this tangible record of each student's performance, two important results may be expected. The students are encouraged in their study through hearing the positive results of their work and are inspired to apply themselves more diligently. The instructor is enabled to objectively evaluate the work of each student and to apply necessary corrective measures. It is recommended that each student retain his own tape for this activity throughout the period of his voice study. As a student develops over a period of time it is most interesting to have a record of early efforts.

2. Videotaping Students

The videotaping of students as they sing is also a valuable teaching tool in connection with solo performance. However, when the equipment is first used, it may be advisable to videotape the entire class, or sections of the class, without deliberate focus on any one student. In this way the class will become accustomed to the procedure; consequently, each member will have an increased possibility of a relaxed solo performance before the camera. Solo performance is an important evaluative tool both for the student and the instructor. Videotaping the performance makes it doubly so. All aspects of stage deportment, as well as vocal and interpretive growth, can be readily monitored by this means. Mannerisms having to do with walking to the platform, the posture, the hands, facial expressions, or other eccentricities can be discussed with objectivity and corrected without unkindness.

3. Solo Performance

During each class some opportunity for solo performance should always be provided. Due to limitations of time, this may be no more than one phrase of a song sung in turn with other members of the class. However, each student should sing an entire song before the class several times during each semester. These solo opportunities offer positive values both for the student and for the instructor. A student's knowledge that he or she may be asked to perform alone provides a powerful motivation for the careful study of each song. Moreover, solo performance enables the student to develop poise and self-confidence before a friendly audience of peers. With growing confidence the student is enabled to develop the ability to project the mood of the song and to sing with some interpretive power.

When each student has a turn at solo performance, whether it be but a phrase within a song or a complete song, the instructor should make a brief but positive commentary. It is well to reinforce student performance at every opportunity, as kindly approval of effort will encourage students to further accomplishment.

4. Evaluation

The final period of each semester might very well take the form of an evaluated performance. Each student can be responsible for the performance of at least three songs from the *Source Book*. Such a performance enables them to have the satisfaction of a mini-recital appearance before their peers as well as a feeling of positive accomplishment. Should it be feasible, this performance could be recorded in order to provide the students with a record of their achievement.

5. Out-of-Class Activities

Students in voice classes should be encouraged to attend at least two professional "events" featuring serious vocal music during each semester. These may be solo recitals, an oratorio, an opera, or a choral concert in which solo artists perform. Through attendance at such events the students become acquainted, even to a limited extent, with the professional vocal world outside the school. They become familiar with the names of prominent vocalists and the variety of their voice classifications. They learn first hand the meaning of artistry and take the first steps in the development of some sense of discrimination. In the event that a school is located away from a major center of musical activity, this requirement, of course, cannot be expected. However, students should be expected to take advantage of every opportunity to hear visiting artists, faculty recitals, and advanced student recitals.

A useful assignment is the writing of a short reaction paper after attending a vocal concert. The effort of responding in writing to the music heard, to the voice or voices, and to the interpretive aspects as well as to performance etiquette is a valuable experience for students. Not only is careful listening assured but the students are enabled to more readily translate such responses into their own performance efforts.

On Practice

Early in the course of study the need for and the importance of judicious outside practice must be established. As obtains in the study of any musical instrument, constant and guided practice is necessary in order to develop the desirable physical responses required for musical needs. Through thoughtful practice, and not mere repetition, the student is enabled to grow in the ability to analyze physical responses and the effect these have on tonal development.

The habits of viable practice must be set in class.

The moderate routinization of the class period should be adopted by the students for their practice periods. The vocalises should be practiced in the order recommended in the *Source Book,* as they are so planned to provide for the developmental growth of vocal tone. Work on the assigned song, already introduced in the class, should follow the vocalise practice. The student should be cautioned, however, to limit practice to short but frequent periods of time in order to avoid the possibility of vocal strain due to an uncoordinated vocal mechanism. Also, in the short practice period a greater possibility exists for concentrated effort. As the instrument gradually develops these periods may be lengthened.

On Studying Songs

In the study of songs, economy of effort should be stressed. In following a definite study pattern, material may be learned quickly and easily, resulting in more time for interpretive growth as well as technical development. Following a discussion of text meanings and the musical aspects as described earlier, a useful plan for individual study should be considered.

The student should first study each song as a whole, taking care that all musical aspects are precisely correct. The short stylistic features accompanying each song in the *Source Book* should be helpful at this time. Secondly, it would be useful to write out the text in order that it may be studied and memorized apart from the score. Also, it may be helpful to study the text in relation to the melodic rhythm. This particular device is especially beneficial for complex rhythmic passages. Thirdly, the melody should be memorized apart from the musical score. The use of a neutral vowel or the text itself could be utilized for this step in the study process. In any case, frequent rechecking of the musical score for the avoidance of any possibility of musical error is strongly recommended. Lastly, each student should be urged to work with an accompanist. In so doing, the student is enabled to solidify the learning process, memorize the accompaniment by ear, and grow in self-confidence as well as interpretive ability.

The specific study suggestions accompanying each song in Part III of the *Source Book* should be carefully considered in connection with any plan of study, as they could be of considerable aid to the student in tonal as well as technical development.

Part II
On Vocal Development

Basically, the act of singing implies the use of the voice as an instrument that is capable of performing music written for the voice, with tonal beauty as well as interpretive capabilities. In order to develop a sonorous and beautiful voice capable of service to the musical art, the singer must perfect the physical coordination of all parts of the mechanism. Understandably, perfection of this coordination cannot be attained in the progress of one year of study in the voice class, nor should this be the goal. However, the concept of the interrelatedness of each part of the vocal mechanism to every other part can be understood and applied to selected songs within the confines of two semesters of class voice. In that relatively short time, the student can also build a firm foundation for future study, should this prove to be desirable.

Part II of the *Source Book* incorporates an empirical approach to the fundamentals of vocal technique in nontechnical language. The succinct but complete explanations of the physical aspect of the singing act are intended to give the youthful student an understanding and an appreciation of the need for a technique in the interpretation of the literature. Judicious attention to these basic principles and their application to the Specific Study Suggestions found in Part III of the *Source Book* will be beneficial and should aid in the vocal growth and development of the student. These will provide the necessary guided repetitiveness for the conditioning of the physical responses in order that the organism be enabled to function in the service of the interpretation of song. It must be reiterated that the perfection of the physical coordination necessary for a perfectly balanced tone cannot be expected within the confines of one year of class voice study. However, a solid foundation can be laid, enabling the student to have a clear understanding of the vocal mechanism as well as an awareness of the capacity of the human voice as a musical instrument.

On Posture

The foundation of a workable singing technique is the posture of the body during the act of singing. The importance of this first step cannot be overemphasized. Good posture facilitates deep breathing and a body that is coordinated and responsive to vocal needs. Every lesson, as well as all practice sessions, should begin with a rethinking of the principles of basic posture.

Correct posture for singing is nothing more than the perfect alignment of the body in a standing position. Every part of the body must be coordinated and involved to facilitate good posture: the feet, the torso, the head. The singer should be conscious of balancing his or her weight firmly on the balls of both feet and, at the same time, keeping the heels firmly on the ground. The chest should be held normally high and the back kept straight. The extension of the spinal column into the skull gives the singer the clue to the correct manner of holding the head. If the singer considers that the spinal column must be kept straight and "stretched" the head will then be correctly balanced on the body. A

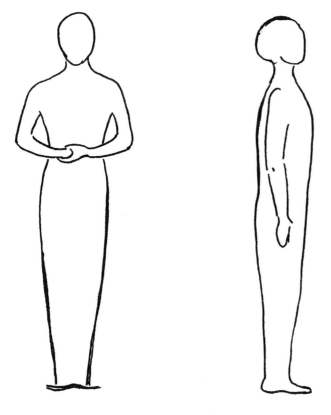

Correct Posture (front and side views).

loose and flexible jaw is easily attainable once the student senses the correct balance of the head.

Specific Study Suggestions

1. **The Feet.** Stand erect while balancing the weight of the body on the balls of the feet. Care must be exercised to avoid throwing the weight of the body to one or the other foot. At all times both feet must be firmly on the ground. For the sake of appearance, the feet should not be too far apart (about seven or eight inches) but one foot may be positioned slightly ahead of the other.

2. **The Chest.** The chest should be held comfortably high. One who is used to slouching may need special help in order to acquire the sensation of the high chest. It is suggested that the arms be extended straight out from the shoulders. While in this position attempt to bring the arms together behind the back. This motion should lift the chest to the desired position, upon which the singer may then drop the arms to the sides of the body.

3. **The Shoulders.** The shoulders must be maintained in a level position during the act of singing. Hunching of the shoulders upward must be avoided, as this brings tension into the neck area. In dropping the arms to the sides of the body one should sense a reach for the floor. By this means one will better understand the admonition to "lower the shoulders."

4. **The Back.** The back must be held erect. To achieve an erect or "stretched" back it is helpful to tighten the abdominal and gluteal muscles. The tightening of these muscles should result in correct pelvic alignment. For a better understanding of this concept it is helpful to place the left arm in the small of the back and push out against the arm. In order to accomplish this act the lower abdominal muscles and the gluteal muscles must be tightened. Or, stand against a wall and attempt to flatten the lumbar section of the spine against the wall. In order to accomplish this act the same muscles must be tightened. Or, stretch out on the floor and force the lumbar section of the spine against the floor. Each of these three suggestions may be helpful in achieving an understanding of the correct pelvic alignment so necessary for erect posture.

5. **The Head.** The head must be perfectly balanced on the body. In order to become aware of this balanced sensation it is helpful to imagine being pulled upwards by a string attached to the crown of the head. This sensation reinforces an understanding of the "stretched" spinal column and the comfortably high chest.

6. **The Jaw.** Once the sensation of the perfect balance of the head on the torso is established, the question of the easy jaw takes care of itself. The jaw must be continuously easing during the act of singing. It is helpful to imagine that one is being "pulled up" behind the ears toward the crown of the head in order to attain the correct sensation of the easy jaw.

Not only is an understanding of these principles of erect posture of first importance in the study of singing, but this understanding is also important for the maintenance of vital health. The mastery of a good posture should be developed slowly over a period of some months.

At no time should postural development be forced, as rigidity could develop.

On Breathing

The act of breathing is a perfectly natural function of the living organism. Breathing for singing, however, requires disciplined control of the breath in order to develop the capacity to sing musical phrases in a musical manner.

Good posture is a prerequisite for a correct breath mechanism. As stated earlier, the body must be perfectly aligned according to the rules for posture. The chest must be held normally high in order that the lungs will have sufficient room for expansion on the breath intake. With this posture the singer will be enabled to take in his or her breath from the diaphragm without any involvement of the chest. It must be pointed out that the high chest breath with heaving shoulders (clavicular breathing) is an anathema to the possibility of good singing. This type of breathing is very limited and tends to tighten the neck muscles, which, in turn, adversely affects the quality of the tone being emitted.

The diaphragm is a very strong convex muscle in the trunk of the body, which separates the lungs and heart from the organs located in the lower part of the torso. It is attached to the sternum, the lower ribs, and the backbone. Upon the intake of breath the diaphragm descends, which is externally evidenced by the expansion of the lower rib cage to which it is attached, and by the expansion of the epigastrium.

Simultaneously with the intake of breath with the diaphragm, the support of the breath must begin. The lower abdominal muscles slowly begin to pull upward in order to steady and support the diaphragm, which, in turn, makes possible a slow and steady expiration of the breath. The lower abdominal muscles continue their pull throughout the musical phrase in resistance to the diaphragm, thus contributing to the continuous expansion of the intercostal muscles of the lower rib cage (see Fig. 2). At no time should the chest be permitted to rise higher than the degree established by good posture. As both the diaphragm and the muscles of the lower rib cage are involved in the singing mechanism, correct breathing for singing is termed *diaphragmatic-costal.*

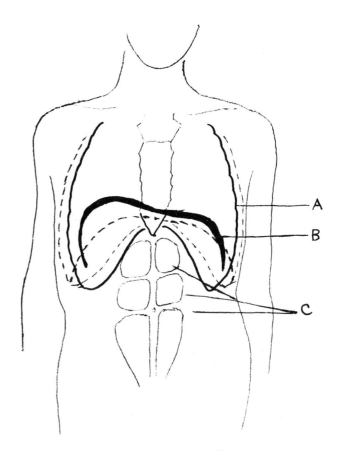

Diaphragm and Lower Abdominal Muscles. A: rib cage; B: diaphragm; C: lower abdominal muscles.

Specific Study Suggestions

1. **Location of the Diaphragm.** The diaphragm itself cannot actually be felt externally by the singer because it is located inside the torso. However, the action of this muscle can be felt in the upper part of the abdomen called the epigastrium, where the lower ribs curve toward the back. Place one hand on the epigastrium and gently cough. Coughing is of no benefit to the vocal mechanism but can be used in this instance as an aid in locating the diaphragm (see Fig. 3).

2. **Breathing from the Diaphragm.** Upon the intake of the breath through slightly parted lips, the epigastrium (upper part of the abdomen) and the lower rib cage should expand. This expansion should take place without any chest involvement whatsoever. Place both hands around the lower

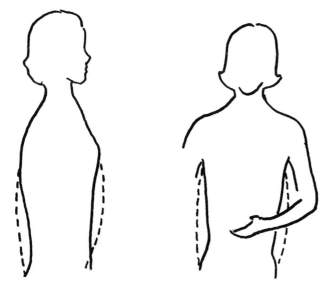

Location of the Diaphragm.

rib cage, the fingers pointing to the spinal column, and take a deep breath, feeling the expansion of the rib cage without chest involvement.

A second means for achieving the sensation of a breath intake without chest involvement would be to place one hand on the epigastrium and the other hand on the chest. Inhale without any chest movement or any unnecessary sound. Breath intake in this manner will result in the expansion of the diaphragm area. Should difficulty persist in the use of the diaphragm, lie on the floor, place one hand on the diaphragm area and breathe normally. As it is not possible to use the chest in breathing while in a supine position, an understanding of "breathing with the diaphragm" will become more clear.

3. **Support of the Diaphragm.** In order to better understand and sense the upward pull of the lower abdominal muscles (see Fig. 2) as they support (or resist) and steady the diaphragm, press the palms of the hands tightly together. Use only the muscles of the forearms, in order to avoid hunching the shoulders, and concentrate on the upward pull of the lower abdominal muscles. Or, it may be helpful to pretend to lift a heavy object from the floor. This lifting action can only be accomplished by an involvement of the lower abdominal muscles as well as the muscles in the lumbar region of the back. Or,

stand behind a straight-back chair that is approximately waist high. Press down on the back of the chair, using only the forearm muscles. In so doing, give particular attention to the involvement of the lower abdominal muscles as they steadily pull upward in support of and in resistance to the diaphragm. A further suggestion might be to place one's hand on the diaphragm area while involving the lower abdominal muscles in the steady upward pull. It will be noted that the diaphragm area seems to become continuously stronger throughout the course of the breath if the chest does not lift. With practice, the concept of the necessity of a certain antagonism between the lower abdominal muscles and the diaphragm in order to steady and support the diaphragm will be better understood.

4. **The Quick Breath.** Should it be necessary to take a quick or rapid breath, inhale through slightly parted lips with a very fast spread of the rib cage and without any chest involvement. Following the breath intake, be aware of the upward pull of the lower abdominal muscles as they steady and support the diaphragm.

Coordinating the Mechanism

The physical aspect of the act of singing must be a refined coordination between the posture of the body, the breathing mechanism, and emission of the tone. Not only the vocal organs are involved in the singing act but also the entire body. It is of great importance that the singer develop the sensation of his or her body functioning as an undivided entity while singing.

Although the entire body, including the vocal organs, functions simultaneously while singing, a clearer understanding of the concept of this coordination will be possible if it is considered in two separate areas in the early stages of vocal study. The first area concerns the muscles of the torso and the second area, the open throat. To reiterate, each area must function simultaneously with the other, beginning with the intake of the breath and throughout each phrase, if a beautiful and free tone is to be achieved.

A. The Muscles of the Torso.

Upon the intake of the breath from the diaphragm through slightly parted lips, the jaw must begin to ease back and up toward the crown of the head. Simultaneously, the lower abdominal muscles must begin their pull upward in support of and in resistance to the diaphragm. Simultaneously, the singer must begin to sense a muscular pull in the muscles of the back toward the crown of the head. In other words, the entire torso is involved in a semicircular manner, from the lower abdominal muscles and up the back to the crown of the head without any loss of a sense of muscular resistance in the diaphragm area. Again, upon the intake of the breath, the entire torso, including the head, becomes involved in the singing act. Each part—the jaw, the diaphragm, the lower abdominal muscles, and the muscles of the back—is interrelated and involved. At no time should any rigidity or stiffness prevail. It is important to point out that practice is necessary for the gradual acquisition of an easy and functioning mechanism and for a deepening awareness of the interaction between all parts of the muscles of the torso.

Specific Study Suggestions

1. **The Jaw.** At no time should any tension or rigidity be felt in the jaw, as this would be reflected in the tone itself. As previously stated in connection with posture, it is helpful to imagine being "pulled up" behind the ears toward the crown of the head, in order to attain the correct sensation of the easy jaw. Also, the suggestion may be made to place one finger on the jaw when attacking the tone and holding it there throughout the phrase. This simple action not only allows the singer to "feel" any jaw stiffness but also can be a reminder to keep reinforcing the principles of good posture for the sake of easing the jaw during the act of singing.
2. **The Diaphragm, the Lower Abdominal Muscles and the Back.** Upon the intake of the breath the expansion of the diaphragm area should be felt. Simultaneously, and as the breath is being slowly expended, it should be possible to feel the movement of the lower abdominal muscles flexing or pulling upward in control of the

diaphragm. Thus, the diaphragm remains expanded in a state of resistance to this movement of the lower abdominal muscles.

In order to gain a more clear understanding of this coordinated action, it would be helpful to place the right hand on the diaphragm area and the left hand on the lower abdomen. As the strengthening, or resistance of the diaphragm is felt under the right hand, notice the easing or flexing action of the lower abdominal muscles under the left hand. As this muscular action is felt, be aware of the progressive involvement of the muscles of the back as they ease upward toward the back of the neck.

To reiterate, the breathing mechanism cannot be isolated from the other parts of the torso. This muscular involvement of the abdomen, diaphragm, back, neck, and head is always an easy, coordinated muscular movement. At no time should there be any straining or unnatural tensing of these muscles. As in any physical activity, regular practice will develop the coordinated mechanism.

B. The Open Throat.

In order to achieve the ideal of the open throat necessary for tonal resonance, it is important to lift and stretch the soft palate as much as possible in order to achieve a maximum pharyngeal opening. Should the soft palate not rise it is impossible for the singer to utilize the resonance cavities of the head. Furthermore, the stretch of the soft palate aids the singer in attaining a greater range extension without any forcing whatsoever. However, the soft palate cannot be voluntarily controlled when singing except by means of the perfection of the pronunciation of the vowels themselves. Purity of the vowels is the impelling force for attaining a maximum pharyngeal opening. The following study suggestions can be of help in efforts to experience the sensation of the open throat.

Specific Study Suggestions

1. **The Mouth.** It is important to remember that the mouth need not be open inordinately wide during the act of singing. Should the mouth

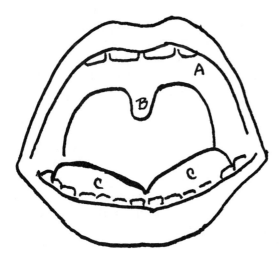

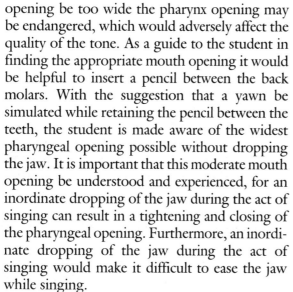

Open Throat (front view). A: soft palate; B: uvula; C: tongue.

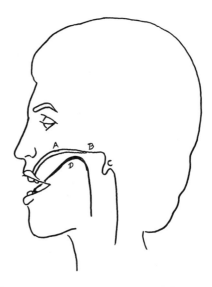

Open Throat (side view). A: hard palate; B: soft palate; C: uvula; D: tongue.

opening be too wide the pharynx opening may be endangered, which would adversely affect the quality of the tone. As a guide to the student in finding the appropriate mouth opening it would be helpful to insert a pencil between the back molars. With the suggestion that a yawn be simulated while retaining the pencil between the teeth, the student is made aware of the widest pharyngeal opening possible without dropping the jaw. It is important that this moderate mouth opening be understood and experienced, for an inordinate dropping of the jaw during the act of singing can result in a tightening and closing of the pharyngeal opening. Furthermore, an inordinate dropping of the jaw during the act of singing would make it difficult to ease the jaw while singing.

2. **The Tongue.** The tip of the tongue should be placed against the lower teeth and the tongue itself should lie as flat as possible in the mouth, without tension. The swallowing mechanism should not be involved in the effort to flatten the tongue, as such action only causes the back of the tongue to rise upward and, if anything, close the throat rather than open it. In some cases, students experience difficulty in coordinating the stretch upward of the soft palate with the flattening of the tongue that makes the open throat possible. Should this be so, it could be

helpful to use a hand mirror for self-examination during this aspect of study.

Exercises for the Voice

The regular and daily use of vocal exercises or vocal gymnastics provides a clear and systematic means for the development of the vocal instrument. Their use permits an approach to the voice as a total instrument, and tonal development throughout the entire range is made possible without the added consideration of textual or musical problems. Of themselves, vocal exercises will not effect vocal growth. The thoughtful application of vocal principles is essential. It is only through daily, consistent and careful attention to every detail that the physical coordination of the mechanism will begin to function, resulting in true progress.

A beautiful and balanced tone is dependent upon the development of tonal resonance resulting from a functioning and totally coordinated mechanism. This ideal buoyancy of the body is the result of coordination of the breathing mechanism and posture at the moment of phonation and throughout each phrase. Every instrument has its own resonator, which brings color, brilliance, and carrying quality to the tone. With the voice the problem of the resonator is more obscure, as the singer must utilize the cavities of the body itself as resonators. The cranium, the sinuses, the pharyngeal areas, and the chest are the sounding boards of the singer and s/he must learn to utilize these effectively in order to yield a voice of maximum tonal beauty capable of meeting the interpretive demands of the music.

Through the judicious use of technical exercises incorporating the physical coordination of all parts of the vocal mechanism, a balanced and resonant tone can be developed by every singer. It is important to work on all exercises, in order, and daily, without the expectation of immediate perfection. In the early weeks of study all exercises should be sung without too much detailed corrective work, in order that assurance in singing be gained before work on detail begins. The first exercises are limited to the middle and low range and make minimal demands on the voice. Each succeeding exercise, while none is long, gradually extends the range and makes progressively greater demands on the vocal mechanism.

All exercises should be sung in unison in the class. Certain low voices, male and female, may experience difficulty in the higher extensions of the exercises. Those students should avoid any strain and simply drop out momentarily.

Exercise 1

HM

The use of an unforced hum is a valuable aid in attaining the sensation of correct mask resonance, and encourages its development. It should be noted that male voices will sound an octave lower than the indicated pitches due to the size of the larynx.

Specific Study Suggestions

1. Begin this exercise on d^1 as indicated and transpose it upward chromatically to c^2. Any voice experiencing difficulty toward the end of the exercise should drop out.
2. The lips should be closed over slightly parted teeth. Avoid any muscular tension in the lips whatsoever.
3. The tip of the tongue should rest against the lower teeth while the back or base of the tongue should be relaxed.
4. Be conscious of easing the jaw while humming and making certain that the jaw continues to ease on the descending tones as well as the ascending tones.
5. Direct the tone to the center of the upper lip. Placing one forefinger on this area is helpful in achieving a sense of the mask resonance without force and directing the tone toward it.
6. Consciously flare the nostrils while humming. By doing this the singer can develop a greater awareness of openness in the pharynx area.
7. Avoid any use of the NG or palate sound in humming. This sound is the result of a tightened tongue muscle; singing with such a condition can result in extreme vocal fatigue and throat strain after a period of time.

Exercise 2

AYE _ _ AH _ _ _ _ _ _ _ _

The use of the three-tone exercise for the middle of the voice enables the singer to begin the warm-up in the simplest possible manner. The vowel AYE should be pronounced as from the naso-pharynx area without any tongue involvement, enabling the singer to attain maximum height and resonance in the tone. In the transition to the AH the singer should maintain the tonal height and resonance of the AYE.

Specific Study Suggestions

1. Begin the exercise on c[1] as indicated and transpose it upward chromatically to a[2]. Any

voice experiencing discomfort toward the last figures should drop out.
2. Maintain correct posture and breath control.
3. As the scale ascends, sense the vowel itself ascending the pharynx area. On the descending portion of the scale maintain the sensation of the ascending vowel as an aid to good pitch.
4. Occasionally place the Mm before the AYE (MAYE) in order to clearly direct the tone into the mask for purposes of gaining an unforced mask resonance.

Exercise 3

The use of the descending scale is particularly helpful in developing extension of the lower voice, both male and female. Also, this exercise is an aid in developing a good sense of pitch in descending the scale. The attack on AYE in the naso-pharynx area, with a full tone, permits the maximum flexing upward of the soft palate. This tone should be briefly held while softening in intensity in order to secure, consciously, greater mask resonance. Without taking a breath, the vowel should blend into an AH for the descent of the scale. Care should be exercised for the maintenance of a very high vowel pronunciation as well as the continuous upward flexion of the soft palate. Thus, the sensation of the tonal placement in the naso-pharynx area on the descending scale can be

retained in order to develop a smooth blending of the middle and chest registers.

Specific Study Suggestions

1. Begin this exercise on c[2] as indicated and transpose it downward chromatically as far as practicable.
2. Sense the easing of the jaw on the tonal attack of the vowel AYE.
3. Consciously lift the soft palate on the AYE and maintain this flexing action throughout the scale descent.
4. The use of a pencil between the back molars is a helpful reminder to maintain the stretch of the soft palate during the scale descent.

Exercise 4

The use of the five-tone scale enables the singers to extend their range gradually and, at the same time, develop flexibility. The attack of the AYE on the quarter notes should be pronounced as from the oro-pharynx area. As the scale ascends the singer should sense not only the tonal ascent in the pharynx but the continuous stretch of the soft palate. Care must be exercised to retain this height as the scale descends, which will be helpful in attaining a smooth transition, or legato, between tones. All weight should be eliminated from the voice in singing the sixteenth notes, and an effort should be made to retain resonance as well as ideal vowel pronunciation in the piano passage.

Specific Study Suggestions

1. Begin the exercise on d^1 as indicated and transpose it upward chromatically to c^2. Should any singer experience discomfort toward the last figures, s/he should drop out. Given time, all voices should experience range extension with the use of this exercise.
2. Maintain correct posture and breath control.
3. Place one forefinger on the jaw as a reminder to maintain its easing at all times.
4. Occasionally place the Mm before AYE (MAYE) to aid in sensing an unforced mask resonance.
5. Consciously strive for a smooth connection between tones by means of the coordination of the mechanism.
6. Exercise the utmost care on the descending passages of the exercise, making certain that the tone retains its pitch and resonance.

Exercise 5

AH

The use of the repeated octave scale is intended as a beginning study in bridging the middle and upper registers of the voice, as well as a study in velocity. Many voices, male and female, have problems in singing from a low point in the range to a higher point and vice versa. The adjustment that must be made in singing a scale of some length over an extended range is essentially one of maintaining maximum resonance throughout the scale in order to eliminate "breaks" in quality.

By careful attention to the coordination of the mechanism a smooth and unbroken scale line can be developed. The vowel AH itself is most important. In ascending the scale, the AH must gradually be "sharpened" or modified with AYE in order to attain the highest possible stretch of the soft palate. This stretch or flex is important for the maintenance of openness of the naso-pharynx region for maximum resonation. In other words, the gradual modification from a palatal resonance to a head resonance can only be made through the gradual modification of the vowel AH to AYE in the scale ascent to the upper reaches of the voice. Every advantage of space in the naso-pharynx area and every advantage of height in the vowel pronunciation must be continually maintained on the descending aspect of the scale for continuing clarity in the scale pattern.

Specific Study Suggestions

1. Begin the exercise on c^1 as indicated and transpose it upward chromatically to a^2. The male voices should begin using the falsetto to effect a mixed registration before it is felt to be absolutely necessary. With careful attention to the coordination of the mechanism, all voices should develop velocity with clarity, and continued range extension.
2. Maintain correct posture and breath control throughout the exercise.

3. Occasionally place one forefinger on the jaw as a reminder to maintain the ease at all times.
4. Attack the initial tone of the scale without weight

and with a heightened vowel pronunciation for greater ease in range extension.

Exercise 6

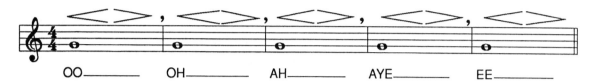

OO_____   OH_____   AH_____   AYE_____   EE_____

The use of this exercise is important for the development of a correct mask placement in the middle of the voice. Furthermore, its mastery will mean the mastery of the vocal instrument and the singer will be enabled to come to a full understanding of the coordination of the mechanism. This total coordination enables the tone itself to gain the desired balance of height, depth, and breadth for maximum beauty.

The vowels of any language provide the sustained aspect of that language. Each vowel must be sung with a pure pronunciation, as any distortion would affect the quality and possibly the pitch of the tone. In order to sing a pure vowel a complete pharyngeal opening (the easing upward of the soft palate) must be maintained with an absolute minimum of tongue involvement. In other words, there must not be any dependence on the tongue for vowel pronunciation as in the spoken vowel; rather, the vowel must be sung as though from the naso-pharynx area without conscious use of the tongue. The soft palate must be continually easing upward and the tongue completely uninvolved in order to permit the tone to travel unhindered from the point of phonation to the resonance chambers of the mask.

In singing the OO vowel the lips must be rounded but relaxed above the easy jaw. The upper lip especially should be "like jelly." The tip of the tongue should rest against the lower teeth, the back of the tongue should remain as low as possible and a conscious effort should be made to stretch the soft palate as high as possible. The singer should sense the point of origin for the vowel as in the naso-pharynx area. Thus, all obstruction from the point of phonation is removed and the vowel is permitted to resonate freely in the mask.

In singing the OH vowel, maintain the shape of the lips used in singing the OO but with a slight easing of the upper lip. The tongue should remain in the same position as for the OO. The singer should sense the point of origin for the OH vowel as being slightly higher in the naso-pharynx area than for the OO.

In singing the AH vowel the shape of the lips should relax slightly from that for the OH. The tongue should remain in the same position as for the preceding vowels and the soft palate must be stretched as high as possible. It is important that the singer refrain from any dropping of the jaw to make space. Rather, the jaw must be continuously easing back and up toward the crown of the head. The singer should sense the point of origin for the AH as being slightly higher in the naso-pharynx area than for the OH. By nature, the AH vowel is low and, therefore, it is imperative that the singer continue sensing the ease in the soft palate in order to maintain height, depth, and breadth in the tone.

In singing the AYE vowel the shape of the lips scarcely changes from that for the AH. It is particularly important in singing the AYE, that the back of the tongue remain as low as possible and the soft palate continue its upward stretch for the retention of a maximum opening in the pharynx area and the avoidance of "pinching" of the tone. The jaw must be continuously easing back and up toward the crown of the head during phonation. The singer should sense the point of origin for the vowel as being slightly higher in the naso-pharynx area than for the AH. In this manner the AYE will maintain height, depth, and breadth in the equal proportions necessary for an ideal pronunciation.

In singing the EE vowel the shape of the lips should

not differ from that for the AYE. The tongue should continue to remain as low as possible, the soft palate must be continuously easing upward, and the jaw must be continuously easing back and up. The singer should sense the point of origin for the EE vowel as being still higher in the naso-pharynx area than for the AYE, in order to attain the ideal tonal focus.

Regardless of the vowel being sung, it should be remembered that the vowels should originate and resonate in the naso-pharynx area without any interference by the tongue. The use of the lips without any jaw involvement whatsoever is extremely important in singing the vowels. However, there should never be any exaggeration of lip movement, as this could affect the resonation and thus the tonal line.

Specific Study Suggestions

1. Begin this exercise on g^1 as indicated. Each vowel should be attacked softly, and gradually swelled to a forte, followed by a gradual decrescendo to the piano of the attack. Take a breath and repeat each vowel as indicated. Transpose the exercise upward chromatically to c^2. Upon the completion of this upward series, run the vowels together on one breath beginning on c^2, take a breath and repeat on b^1, etc., transposing downward chromatically to g^1.

2. Maintain full support of the diaphragm throughout this exercise.

3. Sing with as much mouth closure as possible. The occasional use of a pencil between the back molars is helpful as a reminder to maintain a stretched and lifted soft palate without undue mouth opening.

4. Occasionally flare the nostrils during phonation as an aid to gaining greater consciousness of the pharynx opening.

5. Occasionally place one forefinger against the lower jaw as a reminder to continually ease the jaw in singing from vowel to vowel.

6. When singing the OO vowel, occasionally press both forefingers to the sides of the upper lip with a gentle massaging motion as a reminder to keep the upper lip totally relaxed.

Exercise 7

AH _ _ _ _ _ _ _

The use of the staccato arpeggio is most helpful, for a number of reasons. It can strengthen the diaphragm muscle through disciplined use and develop its control. It can develop a sense of the relationship between the diaphragm and the point of phonation and is useful in the development of tonal height. In the use of the staccato there is no time for the singer to consciously tighten the throat muscles; consequently, it is valuable for the development of range in every voice classification. The male singer will find this exercise especially helpful in developing the ability to blend into the falsetto with ease. Also, its use encourages tonal lightness, pitch acuity, and spontaneity of response in the singer, as well as agility throughout the entire compass of the voice.

Specific Study Suggestions

1. Begin this exercise on c^1 as indicated, transposing it upward chromatically as high as possible without strain.

2. It is helpful to place one hand on the diaphragm area and simulate panting in order to better understand the muscular action necessary for staccato singing.

3. It is helpful for attaining a clear and precise attack to place an "H" before each tone of the scale in the early period of study.

4. Make certain to pronounce the vowel AH very high (no semblance of the UH sound) at the beginning of the scale and to maintain this height throughout the scale.

Exercise 8

AH

One of the difficult problems in developing an easy flowing scale over a long range lies in the tendency to control the tone with the neck muscles and to force the tone upward. This problem can be alleviated by beginning each figure of this exercise with the staccato, as the singer is then encouraged to translate this ease to the legato aspect of the exercise. Also, this exercise is helpful for pitch acuity, for agility, and for the development of an extended range.

Specific Study Suggestions

1. Begin this exercise on c^1 as indicated, transposing it upward chromatically as high as possible without strain.
2. At first, practice this exercise slowly but with a steady tempo. As facility is acquired, gradually pick up the tempo but never so rapidly as to lose pitch acuity.
3. Attack the beginning tone of the scale lightly, making certain that the vowel AH is pronounced very high in the naso-pharynx area. This height of the vowel should be maintained throughout the scale to enable the singer to sweep over the top of the scale and return to the point of attack with ease.
4. Carefully observe the principle of the ease of the jaw, as any rigidity in this area compromises tone quality.
5. Never force the upper limits of the voice. Study to gain the sensation of an even scale from the point of attack to the point of release.

Exercise 9

AYE _____   AH _____

From the earliest weeks of vocal study it is important to work over the entire compass of the voice. The singer should strive to develop flexibility, pitch acuity, and range extension. The use of this long, legato scale is helpful in the achievement of these goals as well as in developing the correct sensations of tonal placement for the highest tones in the range. As stated earlier, it is necessary to gradually "sharpen" the AH or mix it with AYE when ascending the scale, in order to attain the maximum stretch of the soft palate. Furthermore, this exercise is valuable for a continuing and developing awareness of the total coordination of the physical mechanism necessary for the act of singing.

Specific Study Suggestions

1. Begin this exercise on c^1 as indicated, transposing it upward chromatically as high as possible, without strain.
2. The attack on the first tone of the scale should be with a heightened vowel pronunciation. Sense the placement of the vowel on the lowest tone of the scale as on the same level as the highest tone. Retain this height on the descending passage of the scale. Avoid any semblance of overweighting the tone on the attack.
3. Sing this exercise with a moderately forte tone.
4. In the early period of study take a moderate

tempo when working on this exercise. Pick up the tempo only when it can be kept steady.

5. Should any "break" be encountered in the vocal line when ascending the scale, make certain to lift above it by consciously modifying the vowel pronunciation toward an AYE.

Conclusion

The development of a vocal instrument capable of serving the needs of the music can be achieved by the systematic and daily use of the preceding exercises while applying careful attention to every detail of the coordination of the vocal mechanism. In the class period the coordination of the mechanism should be the particular concern of the instructor. The empirical explanations of each facet of the singing act included in the *Source Book* are intended as reinforce-

ment of the teacher's explanations and for reference use by the student during practice time.

The basic principle of good vocal tone production is essentially very simple. If the two parts of the vocal mechanism—the muscles of the torso (including the breathing mechanism) and the open throat—are perfectly coordinated and vowels are perfectly pronounced, a balanced tone will result. A balanced tone is one having tonal height, tonal breadth, and tonal depth in equal proportions. Guided and constant repetition over a period of some years is necessary before the singer can expect to have mastery over his or her instrument. However, in the period of time given to voice work in a class situation (generally one year), the student-singer can expect to have a good understanding of the mechanism, a certain insight as to the application of these learnings, and some knowledge of repertoire.

Part III
The Songs

The songs in this collection were selected for use in conjunction with the procedures recommended in Parts I and II. Not only were the songs selected from the range of the history of the American art song, which embodies a variety of compositional techniques and vocal styles, but the particular needs of the young singer were also noted. These considerations included moderate length, simplicity in terms of compositional techniques, a range not exceeding a–g^2, and the tessitura not exceeding d^1–d^2.

The chronological arrangement of songs by birth date of each composer not only emphasizes the significance of each composer in the history of the American art song but also precludes the grading of the songs by level of difficulty. In the opinion of the writer, an arbitrary grading of materials is, at best, an artificial limitation and does not allow either the instructor or the student sufficient flexibility in the choice of songs for study.

Following each song a biographical sketch of the composer is presented, as well as a brief discussion of the stylistic and aesthetic features of each song. Also provided are specific study suggestions with reference to interpretation and to the vocal technique procedures recommended in Parts I and II.

Bibliographical references to, and quotations from, the work of other writers may be found in the *Selected Sources,* pp. 174–175.

MY DAYS HAVE BEEN SO WONDROUS FREE

Francis Hopkinson, 1737-1791
Arr. by Walter Kob

Francis Hopkinson

Francis Hopkinson, a remarkably versatile and distinguished man, was born in Philadelphia on September 21, 1737, and died there on May 9, 1791. He was a patriot in the fullest sense and was active in every aspect of Philadelphia's intellectual life. He was a delegate to the Continental Congress and a signer of the Declaration of Independence. A lawyer who became the first judge of the Admiralty Court in Pennsylvania, he was a fluent writer of political pamphlets and satirical poems, which were influential in forming the public opinion of his time.

Not only was Hopkinson famous in the political and literary life of his time but he was also a patron of the arts, who played the organ and harpsichord and composed a number of musical works. As a composer he was known for his church music, various instrumental works, and especially his songs. Undoubtedly many of his works have been lost but fourteen songs are known. His distinction lies in the fact that he was the first American-born composer to write an art song in America. That Hopkinson himself was conscious of the significance of this accomplishment can be deduced from the conclusion of the dedicatory letter that accompanied the first eight songs, sent to his friend, George Washington:

> However small the Reputation may be that I shall derive from this Work I cannot, I believe, be refused the Credit of being the first Native of the United States who has produced a Musical Composition.

Stylistic Features

"My days have been so wondrous free," to a text by Thomas Parnell, was scored by the composer as a melody with unfigured bass. According to the style of the time, the harpsichordist was expected to "fill in" the harmonies, including improvisation using appropriate imitations, nonharmonic tones, etc. The arrangement used in this *Source Book* is based on a photographic reproduction of the original manuscript. All notational details have been retained, including barrings, ornamentation, spelling, and punctuation in the text. However, the original key of A Major has been transposed to F Major in order that the range might be reasonable for young voices.

"My days have been so wondrous free" has the simplicity of a folk song. The lyrical melody paints the bright text appropriately; the melismatic setting of such words as "wondrous" in measure 10, "birds" in measure 13, "careless" in measure 15, and "waters" in measure 29 underlines their poetic meanings.

Specific Study Suggestions

This spirited song should be performed lightly and lyrically with a clearly enunciated text in the English folk-style tradition. Two important points for study are presented in this song: the ascending leaps in the melodic line found in measures 9, 22, 30, 37, 43, and the ascending scalewise passage in measure 41.

—Sing the lower tone of each ascending leap softly in order to avoid over-weighting the lower tone of the interval in each case.
—Vocalize the passage in which the leap is located on a neutral vowel for development of beauty of line.
—Sing the passage with the text, striving to attain the same legato.
—Never permit the consonants to interfere with the flow of the tone.
—Discuss the melodic phrasing indicated by Hopkinson as an aid in understanding the melismatic setting, as in measures 10, 13, 15, etc.
—Discuss dynamic possibilities in keeping with the style, as none has been indicated by the composer.

To my sister, Evelyn Hickle

When Jesus Wept

"A Canon of 4 in 1."   An Easter Song for Medium Voice   William Billings
Transcribed and edited
by Gordon Myers

flowed___ be - yond all bound; When Je - sus groaned,___ a
point - ed the way di - vine; When Je - sus spake,___ in

trem - bling fear Seiz'd all___ the guil - ty world___ a - round.
ev - ery place The heaven - ly spi - rit there___ did shine.)

3. When Je - sus wept,___ the fall - ing tear In mer - cy
(When Je - sus knelt___ up - on___ the ground, The light of

flowed___ be - yond all bound; When Je - sus groaned,___ a
heaven___ shone ev - ery - where; When Je - sus prayed,___ the

trem - bling fear Seiz'd all - the guil - ty world___ a - round.
ho - ly sound of an - gel voic - es filled___ the air.)

4. When Je - sus wept,___ the fall - ing tear In mer - cy

flowed___ be - 'yond all bound; When Je - sus groaned, ___ a

trem - bling fear Seiz'd all___ the guil - ty world___ a - round.

William Billings

A great musical personality, William Billings was born in Boston on October 7, 1746, and died there on September 26, 1800. Although not a solo song composer he is included in this collection because of his unique contribution to the development of American vocal music.

Billings came of a poor tradesman's family and was apprenticed as a tanner while still a boy. He must have had an unusual and compelling personality for, in spite of a most unprepossessing appearance, a lack of formal education, and a humble trade, he was a friend of many influential men of his time.

A completely self-taught musician, Billings was famous for his "fuguing tunes." His first publication was the "New England Psalm Singer," which appeared in 1770. Not only was this Billings's first publication but it was also the first sacred music collection composed by a native American. The psalm tunes have been greatly admired by scholars, especially as they are said to represent an anthology of sixteenth-century religious poetry, as well as for the fact that the melodies skillfully reflect the textual meanings.

The Stoughton (Mass.) Musical Society, the oldest musical society still in existence, was organized by William Billings. He was the first director in American history to use the string bass in church services as well as the pitch pipe for use in "striking up the tunes."

Stylistic Features

"When Jesus Wept" first appeared in the *New England Psalm Singer* in 1770 as a round. The arrangement for solo voice used in this *Source Book* provides a suitable accompaniment by placing the canonic entrances in the piano part. Although not composed as a solo song, this inspired melody lends itself to solo performance. The textual implications are portrayed with rare beauty, each word being perfectly and effortlessly incorporated into the flowing melody. The melodic and rhythmic movement for such words as "wept" in measure 2, "falling tear" in measure 3, and "trembling fear" in measure 11 tone-paint the text in such a way that the singer has no question pertaining to interpretation.

Specific Study Suggestions

The successful interpretation of this sensitive song is dependent upon the singer's keen perception of poetic meanings linked to an inspired melody. The technical problem presented by this demand is essentially that of maintaining the tonal flow, the legato, throughout.

—Practice taking quick but unobtrusive breaths at the end of each phrase as indicated in the score. The tone before the breath intake should be judiciously "robbed" in order that the attack on the following tone be precisely in time.
—Class sing original canon on a neutral vowel for the attainment of legato as well as balance between the voices.
—The class situation provides a fine opportunity to sing this song as a round, as the composer originally intended.
—Emphasize the importance of singing from vowel to vowel, not permitting the consonants to interfere in any way, for the development of tonal flow.
—Place one hand on the diaphragm area and, while singing, be aware of a continuous expansion of the area under the hand without any involvement of the chest. This activity should provide for a developing awareness of the resistance between the lower abdominal muscles and the diaphragm necessary for tonal support.

BEAUTIFUL DREAMER
(SERENADE)

Words and Music by STEPHEN C. FOSTER

Beau - ti - ful dream - er, wake un - to me, _____

Star - light and dew drops are wait - ing for thee; _____ Sounds of the rude world

heard in the day, _____ Lull'd by the moon - light have all pass'd a - way! _____

Beau - ti - ful dream - er, out on the sea,

Mer - maids are chaunt - ing the wild lore- lie; O - ver the stream - lot

va - pors are borne, Wait-ing to fade at the bright com - ing morn,

Beau ti - ful dream - er, beam on my heart, E'en as the morn on the

stream-let and sea;_____ Then will all clouds of sor - row de - part,_____

Beau - ti - ful dream - er, a - wake un - to me!_____ Beau - ti - ful dream - er a - wake un - to

ad lib.

me!_____

A tempo.

Stephen Collins Foster

Stephen Foster was born in Lawrenceville, a small town near Pittsburgh, Pennsylvania, on July 4, 1826, and died in New York City on January 13, 1864. Strictly speaking, Stephen Foster was not an "art-song" composer. He was born far from the acknowledged centers of American culture, as the Pittsburgh of that time was still the "frontier." Furthermore, his musical education was negligible. However, he was strongly attracted to the music of his day such as the "shouting" songs of the Negro church services, the songs of the itinerant minstrel shows and the popular parlor ballads. These influences were extremely important in the development of the composer and he utilized elements of all of them in his songs.

Foster composed more than two hundred songs in his short life. His greatest desire was to write songs that would give pleasure, and very early he found the vein of his popularity. His themes were of the people and his musical means were easily understood.

Foster excelled in two types of song: the pure minstrel song and the sentimental ballad. The sentimental ballads, characterized by directness and simplicity, were derived from the English ballads so popular in America, the most famous of which were "Jeanie with the Light Brown Hair" and "Beautiful Dreamer."

Foster had the gift of melody to such an uncommon degree that even with a minimal musical training, his genius captured the essence of the American experience in his own period. In 1940 he was elected to the Hall of Fame at New York University; in 1951 an act of Congress made January 13th the annual Stephen Foster Day; and the University of Pittsburgh has established the Stephen Foster Memorial.

Stylistic Features

"Beautiful Dreamer" was one of Foster's last songs written before his untimely death at age thirty-seven. This sentimental ballad is folk-like in character, with its repetitious but lovely melody and its basic harmonic accompaniment. The text speaks of the "Beautiful Dreamer" asleep to all worldly cares and being serenaded by her lover. The quiet and calm of this mood is portrayed by the monotony of the arpeggiated accompaniment, by the repetitiveness of the melodic pattern, and by the strophic form itself.

Specific Study Suggestions

The unsophisticated charm of this delightful ballad dictates that it be sung in a lyrical, almost folk-like style with as pure and unemotional a quality as possible, avoiding all stresses and exaggerations. The calm and reposeful mood calls for a smooth legato despite the stylistic setting. At the same time the moderate tempo should be maintained without the use of rubato in order to avoid oversentimentalizing the conception. Lovely and unpretentious, "Beautiful Dreamer" presents two particular problems to the student: the syllabic setting in which separate syllables have been set to each note of the melody, and the necessity for a rapid breath intake after every two measures of the song without interrupting the tonal flow.

—Gently conduct, three beats to a measure, while choral-speaking the text. In this way a feeling for the rhythmic swing and the sense of stress and release inherent in the text will be attained.
—Continue the conducting pattern and, at the same

time, vocalize the melody on a neutral vowel such as OO or AH. Thus, the need for a legato approach to the lyricism of the graceful melody, despite the syllabic setting, will become increasingly clear.

—Apply the text. Remember to sing from vowel to vowel, never permitting the consonants to interfere with the legato tonal flow.

—Place the hands around the lower rib cage with the fingers pointed toward the spinal column and practice taking quick breaths through the mouth by rapidly spreading the rib cage without any involvement of the chest. Exercise care on the quick breath intake that the legato line of the melody is undisturbed.

—Discuss the distinction between the melismatic setting of "My days have been so wondrous free" by Hopkinson and the syllabic setting of "Beautiful Dreamer" by Foster.

To Mr. Gardner Lamson.

ALLAH.

Poem by H. W. Longfellow.

G. W. CHADWICK.

Serioso.

Al - lah gives light in dark-ness, Al - lah gives rest in pain,

Cheeks that are white with weep - ing Al - lah paints red a - gain.

The flowers and the blossoms with - er, Years van-ish with fly - ing feet,

George Whitefield Chadwick

George W. Chadwick, a noted educator as well as a composer, was born in Lowell, Massachusetts, on November 13, 1854, and died in Boston on April 4, 1931. After a short period of time in his father's business, he decided to become a music teacher and obtained a position at Olivet College in Michigan. Realizing the need for further musical education, he went first to Leipzig to study under Reinecke and Jadassohn and later to Munich to study under Rheinberger.

After those years of study in Germany, Chadwick returned to the United States in 1880, opened a studio in Boston, and also became organist at the South Congregational Church. In 1882 he was appointed to the faculty of the New England Conservatory and fifteen years later became the school's director, a post he retained until his death. The conservatory flourished and grew under his direction. He was noted for his concern for the students as well as for his attention to the slightest details of the life of the school. Among his students who achieved prominence in the musical life of the United States were Horatio Parker, Sidney Homer, Arthur Whiting, Henry Hadley, Frederick Converse, Daniel Gregory Mason, Edward B. Hill, and William Grant Still.

George Chadwick was a prolific composer in many forms. He composed five operas; three symphonies and other large orchestral works; choral and vocal works with orchestra; chamber music; piano music; and more than one hundred songs in the romantic style of his period. The "Ballad of Trees and the Master," "Bedouin Love Song," "Lochinvar," "The Curfew," and "Allah" are among his most famous and reflect his particular gifts.

Honors conferred on Chadwick during his lifetime included an honorary Master of Arts degree from Yale University in 1897, and an honorary LL.D. from Tufts in 1905. In 1908 he was elected to membership in the American Academy of Arts and Letters, taking the seat vacated by the death of Edward MacDowell. That group awarded him its Gold Medal in 1928.

Stylistic Features

In ternary (ABA) form, "Allah" is a dignified interpretation in song of Henry W. Longfellow's poem expressing the reliance of man throughout life upon his Maker. The sustained melodic line, which is limited in range, supports the textual meanings in all aspects. The low tessitura throughout the song and the low full chords of the accompaniment in the first section are also effective in conveying the sense of seriousness inherent in the elevated mood of the text.

The use of a triplet figure in the melodic line, beginning in measure 7 at the cadence of section A of the song and extending throughout section B, lends interest and rhythmic movement to the otherwise repetitive vocal line. Although diatonic chords prevail throughout the song the occasional chromatic alterations, such as the use of half-diminished chords in measures 6 and 24, provide coloration and stress for the words "weeping" and "vanish." Also, the major cadence chord in measure 16 affords a sudden "surprise" from the expected minor. The arpeggiated version of the chordal accompaniment in the return to the A section of this ternary song in measure 19 is a further variation effectively enhancing poetic meanings.

Specific Study Suggestions

The solemn character or the text of "Allah" is a clear indication to the performer of the composer's interpretive intentions. Although the mood is earnest it need not be projected in a weighty manner but rather with dignity and conviction. Careful attention should be given to tonal support in order to maintain the breadth of tone demanded by the textual message as well as by the fullness of the chordal accompaniment. Also, the repetitive character of the vocal line requires a careful consideration of coloristic contrast within each phrase in the performance of this song.

—Emphasize the importance of rhythmic accuracy in singing the characteristic triplet figure as found throughout the song. Occasionally direct the class to conduct while vocalizing melodic sections incorporating this figure, as an aid in achieving rhythmic accuracy.

—Discuss the need for dynamic contrast in passages that are melodically repetitive, such as in measures 1–2 and 5–6.

—Emphasize the importance of continuing support of the diaphragm. Occasionally vocalize a phrase on a neutral vowel while giving specific attention to the action of the muscles of the torso.

—In measure 6 exercise care in singing "weeping." First, vocalize measures 5–6; second, sing the text, using care to maintain the tonal flow from syllable to syllable. It is important to point out to the class that the necessary consonants in a word must not interfere with tonal flow.

—In measure 24 the distinctively English vowel of the word "vanish" must be kept open and undistorted without any flatness in the pronunciation until the final eighth note of the measure. Vocalize the passage, beginning on measure 23 on a neutral vowel, and transfer the sensation of ease thus attained to the singing of the text.

To Reinald Werrenrath

The Last Song

Hartley Alexander   James H. Rogers

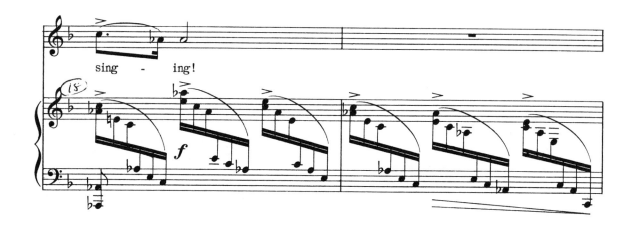

sing - ing!

I would have the winds to en - vel - ope my

bod - y;

I would have the sun to shine up - on my

bod - y;   The

whole world would I have   to make music with me!

James H. Rogers

James H. Rogers, organist and composer, was born in Fair Haven, Connecticut, on February 7, 1857, and died in Pasadena, California, on November 28, 1940. His early musical studies were in Chicago with Clarence Eddy. His great talent was such that at the early age of sixteen, he was sent to Berlin for five years in order to study piano, theory, and organ. His studies were concluded in Paris under Fissot, Guilmant, and Widor. Upon his return to the United States in 1883, Rogers settled in Cleveland as organist at the Euclid Avenue Temple and the First Unitarian Church. He was also active as a music critic for the Cleveland *Plain Dealer* and conductor of the Rubinstein Club. His retirement years were spent in California.

Rogers was notably successful as a composer, with a published catalogue of more than 150 works. The catalogue includes works in various forms, such as Morning and Evening Services, cantatas, part-songs, piano pieces, and organ studies, as well as the songs. His songs are noted for the singability of their graceful melodic lines as well as for the highly pianistic style of the accompaniments.

Stylistic Features

"The Last Song," by James H. Rogers to a text by Hartley Alexander, published in 1922, was a famous song of its day. The through-composed song is an exuberant outpouring in a true nineteenth-century romantic style. The intensity and energy of the composer's setting are reflected both in the melody and the accompaniment. The sustained, syllabic melodic line is of a restricted range with frequent skips of fourths and fifths. The changing tempo indications found throughout, as in measure 12 marked "più mosso," in measure 20 marked "più

agitato," to "ma ben declamando" in measure 37, highlight the ongoing drama of the text. The use of triplet figures in the melodic line, as in measures 5, 16, 35 and 40, and the dotted eighth note figure found in measures 6, 12, 14 and 18 lend further urgency to the setting.

The fullness of the harmonic texture of the piano accompaniment fully supports the drama of the text. Occasional chromatic alterations provide variety to this song in F Major, and effectively highlight the text. The use of an augmented triad in measures 14 and 18 is a rather effective treatment of the word "singing." Also of interest is the composer's deliberate use of many three-measure phrases throughout, dictated no doubt by the poetic rhythms and meter. A brief excursion into A Major in measures 28–32 provides a supportive climax to the text at this point, "The whole world would I have to make music with me."

The coda-like ending that begins in measure 33 utilizes fragments from the song's opening in the text, in the melodic line, and in the full chordal harmonic texture.

Specific Study Suggestions

The inherent excitement of this setting provides the singer with a clear guide as to its interpretation. The melodic rhythmic patterns and the fullness of the harmonic texture are supportive of the text drama. This song is a fine study for the development of a full and supported tone quality, which demands a well-coordinated vocal mechanism.

—Plan the dynamic development of the interpretation with care. Avoid the temptation to overemphasize "forte" singing in this stirring song.

—Simultaneously conduct and choral-speak the text, utilizing the melodic rhythm for rhythmic precision. Especially note triplet patterns and dotted eighth note patterns as found throughout.

—Use care to sustain the melodic half notes for their full value as found in measures 8, 10, 13, 14, etc.

—Take care to avoid any tension in the jaw when working for clarity in text enunciation.

VII.
The Sea.
Das Meer.

Broadly, with rhythmic swing.
Breit, mit rhythmischem Schwung.

Mac Dowell, Op. 47.

D. L-V. 5582.

Edward MacDowell

Edward MacDowell, who was destined to be known as the greatest American composer of the nineteenth century, was born in New York City on December 18, 1861, and died in the same city on January 23, 1908. By the time MacDowell was fifteen years old it was decided that his great talent warranted study in Europe. After concentrated study in composition and piano in Paris, Stuttgart, Wiesbaden, and Frankfurt, MacDowell obtained a position as head of the piano department of the Darmstadt Conservatory. About this time he had the opportunity to play his first piano concerto for Franz Liszt, who was greatly impressed with the young artist. It was Liszt, as well as Joachim Raff of Frankfurt, who influenced MacDowell to devote the major portion of his energies to composition.

After MacDowell's marriage to Marian Nevins in 1884, the two remained in Germany for four years before deciding to make their home in Boston. During the next eight years the composer produced many important works, and with the performance of his first piano concerto in 1888, the public acknowledged his stature as a composer-pianist. This success was assured with the performance of the second piano concerto in New York the following season.

In 1896 MacDowell accepted the offer of President Seth Low of Columbia University to head a new Department of Music. As the many commitments of his Columbia post allowed little time to compose during the school year, MacDowell acquired a small New Hampshire farm in Peterboro in 1896 as a summer retreat for his private work. The serenity of the place was so ideal that the MacDowells envisioned it as a place for creative artists in other areas of the arts as well as music. They believed in the interrelationship among all the arts

and that practitioners in all the arts could benefit greatly through contact with one another.

The MacDowell Association became a reality after the composer's death. Mrs. MacDowell spent the remainder of her long life raising funds, buying additional land, and building studios. The existence of the colony has had a deep and lasting influence on American cultural life through the opportunities afforded artists for beautiful surroundings in which to work.

MacDowell composed orchestral works, concerti, piano solos and duets, and songs. He favored titles, especially in the piano works, that suggested a programme. In his Second Suite, Op. 48, he used Indian melodies for his material. MacDowell wrote forty-two songs. He felt strongly that the text was the most important aspect of a song and that the accompaniment should be a background for the words. Finding that many poems were far too unmusical to set, he wrote the texts for a number of his songs. All of Op. 56, save one, all of Op. 58 and Op. 60, the "Slumber Song" of Op. 9, and three songs of Op. 47—"The Robin Sings in the Apple Tree," "Confidence," and "The West Wind Croons in the Cedar Trees"—were set to his own texts.

Stylistic Features

"The Sea," from the Op. 47, to a text by W. D. Howells, is a composition illustrative of MacDowell's concern for textual nuance. This is a compelling song in which the tragic implications of the text are translated into musical terms. The relentless dotted rhythms of the melody might dramatize the inexorability of the mood as well as the rhythm of the pounding seas. Also, the restricted range of the melody within one octave, with its characteristic scalewise passages interrupted by the octave intervals in measures 7–9 and again in measures 27–28, further emphasizes the desperate emotion of the central character.

The low, full chords of the accompaniment, predominantly spaced two to a measure, give additional support to the mood of immutable hopelessness. The composer's sensitive and judicious use of chromatic harmonies not only points up textual implications in specific words but also delineates the form of the poetic text. The diatonic harmonies of the peaceful opening become increasingly chromatic as the text intensifies, approaching section B at measure 11. The chromatic chords effectively color such words as "dies," "whispering," "mute," and "in vain." Also, the chromatic line in the accompaniment of measures 11–14 not only contributes to the mysterious and evil atmosphere but also points up a kind of acceptance, through the use of a D Major chord on the word "she" in measure 15 as the composer prepares to return to section A.

Specific Study Suggestions

In singing this strongly emotional song the performer need only respond to the composer's imaginative harmonic and melodic treatment of the text for an effective interpretation. The unalterable swing of the rhythm from beginning to end is important to consider as an indication of the ineludible fates of the protagonists.

—Maintain solidity of tone throughout each phrase despite the characteristic rhythmic figure of a dotted eighth note followed by a sixteenth note.
—"Stretch" the sixteenth notes throughout in order to sustain the drama inherent in the forceful text.
—In singing the octave leaps, such as in measure 7, avoid a heavy tone on d^1 in each case in order to maintain the tonal line.
—Maintain full support of the diaphragm throughout the performance of this song. This is especially important in those phrases that lie in the lower reaches of the voice, as in measures 10–14 and again in measures 28 to the end. The dramatic interest is very great in these measures but this impact would be lost should the singer de-vitalize his tone.
—Take in breath every two measures as indicated by the text. An exception might be after "light" in measure 6. Although not textually indicated, a breath at this point is important due to the crescendo on the ascending melodic line.
—Rhythmically choral-speak the text while conducting, in order to sense the broad rhythmic swing.
—Give careful attention to the short melodic appoggiaturas in measures 2, 22, and 32 for expressive purposes.

Sometimes I feel like a Motherless Child

Negro Spiritual
Arranged by

H. T. BURLEIGH

*) The original form of this measure was written the liberty of altering it as above. *H. T. B.*

In order to facilitate vocalization I have taken

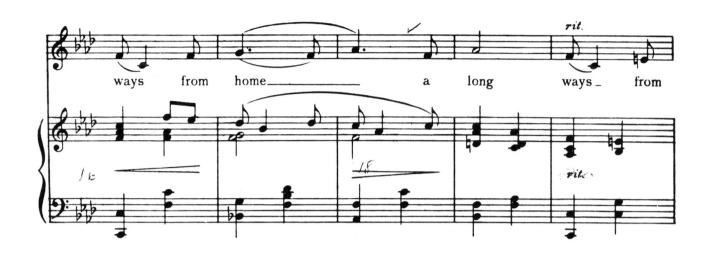

ways   from home_____   a   long   ways_   from

home._____   A   long   ways_   from   home_____

_____   a   long   ways_   from   home._____

Harry (Henry) T. Burleigh

Often referred to as the first of the black nationalistic composers, Harry T. Burleigh was born in Erie, Pennsylvania, on December 2, 1866, and died in Stamford, Connecticut, on September 12, 1949. Burleigh had little formal musical training until his mid-twenties, although he sang professionally in Erie. In 1892 he obtained a scholarship to the National Conservatory of Music in New York, where he studied composition with Dvořák. Other teachers were Rubin Goldmark, John White, and Max Spicker. After arriving in New York, Burleigh continued his singing career and in 1894 obtained a position as baritone soloist at St. George's Church, where he was to remain for fifty-two years. He also held a similar position at Temple Emanu-El in New York from 1900 to 1925. Burleigh was honored during his lifetime with an honorary M.A. degree from Atlanta University and an honorary Mus.D. degree from Howard University.

Burleigh was the first composer to arrange spirituals for the solo voice, thus making them accessible for concert use by the rising school of black performing artists. Although the composer had written numerous art songs and ballads, choral works, and miscellaneous works for the piano and the violin, it was his strong desire to incorporate into his composition the African-American quality, the "humanness" that motivated his early settings of spirituals. In these songs Burleigh captured the essence of the black experience while, at the same time, maintaining the quality of the art song.

Stylistic Features

"Sometimes I Feel Like a Motherless Child" was one of Harry Burleigh's earliest arrangements of a spiritual for the solo voice. The mournful "blues" text depicts the depths of loneliness and isolation felt by the uprooted slave transported far from his home and family to a strange land. The plaintive melody, with its characteristic descending minor third interval, and the motivic repetition for such passages as "motherless child" further emphasize the essentially lonely mood. The melodic line is limited to a range of one octave, and the restricted skips of thirds, fourths, and short descending scalewise passages further carry out the resigned mood of the text.

The tasteful chromatic accompaniment never intrudes upon the dignity of the text, and its chordal style supports the sense of sorrow inherent in the spiritual. The composer provides a change of harmonic texture in the second verse of the strophic melody in order to further underline the textual meanings and to provide the performer with needed support in his interpretation.

Specific Study Suggestions

The designation "lamentoso" is the key to the interpretation of this text. The mournful melody should be sung with some rubato in order to evoke these emotional qualities, and the composer has provided a chordal accompaniment which permits such freedom. The textual and melodic repetiveness of the arrangement are further provision to enhance interpretive intensity, giving the singer wide opportunity for coloristic variation.

It would be well to have a brief discussion about the text. Each line of both stanzas is repeated three times in the setting, thus providing a haunting quality that emphasizes the numbing aspect of lifelong oppression. The victim, unable any longer to feel anger, can only express himself with resignation and so repeat over and over, as would a child, the same phrase.

—Sway the entire torso on the first beat of each measure, while choral-speaking the text. Thus, through feeling the basic beat of one to each measure, the young singer will be enabled to better understand the haunting quality of the text and, at the same time, to sense the rubato needed for the successful interpretation of the spiritual. Also, by employing this means of feeling the rubato, the singer will be made more sensitive to the need for preserving the basic rhythm without distortion. The use of physical responses to the basic beat of the music is helpful, too, in obtaining just the right amount of stress needed for a successful interpretation of such words as "feel," "motherless," and "home."

—Vocalize the melody on a neutral vowel while giving full consideration to basic posture and support, to aid in achieving the legato flow essential for the interpretation of this spiritual.

—Carefully observe and listen for intervallic differences for "sometimes" in measures 3, 7, and 11, and measures 35, 39, and 43, for intonation and for memory.

—Note the composer's use of melodic syncopation as an expressive device in measures 7, 11, 16, 20, etc. Discuss with class the effect of this syncopation in enhancing the poignant mood of the text.

—Carefully observe holding the "o" vowel for its full value for expressive purposes, as found in measures 17–18; 21–22; 25–27; 29–30; 49–50; 53–54; 57–58; 61–62.

AFTERNOON ON A HILL

EDNA ST. VINCENT MILLAY

ARTHUR FARWELL
A.S.C.A.P.

Arthur Farwell

Arthur Farwell, who was destined to play a major part in the musical awakening of America, was born in St. Paul, Minnesota, on April 23, 1872, and died in New York City on January 20, 1952. As a child he did not exhibit any unusual musical talent, nor, as he grew into young manhood, did he express any particular interest in music as a career. It was during his college years, when studying engineering at Massachusetts Institute of Technology, that the concert activity of Boston and his friendship with musicians inspired Farwell to look to music for his life work. He began studying composition with Homer Norris in Boston and upon graduation went to Germany for two years to work with Engelbert Humperdinck and Hans Pfitzner. Also, for a brief time, he studied with Alexandre Guilmant in Paris. Returning to the United States in 1899, Farwell began a fruitful, diversified career that was to include composing, teaching, publishing, writing, criticism, and music promotion.

Farwell's work as an educator began at Cornell University in 1889. During his one year as a lecturer in music at Cornell the composer began his research into Indian music and composed his "American Indian Melodies" for the piano. Farwell's inability to find a publisher and the discovery that many other American composers shared his plight led to the founding of the Wa-Wan Press in his Newton Centre, Massachusetts, home. The expressed goal of the press was to work for the American composer and for American music. Thirty-seven composers were represented in the press. Not all of them were of the top calibre, but the press did establish a forum for American composers who would otherwise be unheard.

In order to further the work of the Wa-Wan Press, Farwell undertook extensive tours throughout the United States between the years 1903 and 1907. He lectured, performed, and "preached the gospel of American music." A further outgrowth of his tours was the establishment of the National Wa-Wan Society of America, with centers in major U.S. cities. Through its bulletin, the society was to provide an editorial platform to arouse America to its own artistic significance and to gain further recognition for the American composer.

There were to be many and divergent activities in the full life and career of Arthur Farwell, but all were related in his destiny and allied him to every aspect of musical life in the United States. He will be remembered as a crusader for the cause of the American composer and his music. He was a doer who composed and published, wrote and evangelized. For generations the American people had been trained to think that only European music was "real," whereas Farwell believed that there could be a true American music—involving the cultural history of America, but still music of universal significance.

Arthur Farwell was a prolific composer in many forms. He wrote pageants and masques including "The Pilgrimage Play" and "Caliban" for performance in amphitheaters in natural surroundings such as the Hollywood Bowl and New York City's Central Park. Orchestral works, concerti, chamber works, piano and instrumental works, choral works, and songs are included in the catalogue of his life work. He composed 127 songs, thirty-nine of which were to Emily Dickinson texts. Other poets favored by the composer included Percy Bysshe Shelley, William Blake, and Edna St. Vincent Millay. His range of compositional expression in the songs was very wide, from the folk quality of his "Folk Songs of the West and South" and his "American Indian

Melodies" to the artistic and emotional power of "Wild Nights! Wild Nights!"

Stylistic Features

"Afternoon on a Hill," one of four songs of Op. 75, to a text by Edna St. Vincent Millay, is a joyous, lighthearted song that reflects the composer's love of nature. The simplicity of this short and animated text is carried out in every aspect of the composition. The "happy" key of G Major is employed, although in measure 11 there is a drift toward D Major for four measures. The melody, restricted to a one-octave range, is folklike in character and very much in keeping with the buoyant, airy mood of the text. Melodic contrast is provided, however, by the lilting, dotted rhythm of the melody in section A and the quiet calm of section B, which begins with measure 11.

The top line of the accompaniment follows the voice throughout except in measures 15–17, where the return to the original key begins. The texture of the accompaniment is never heavy or overweighted, always enhancing the sprightly mood of the text. Colorful chromatic harmonies, such as the use of the chromatic chord for the transition to the tonic on the return to the A section in measure 18, provide richness and energy to the conceptions. Also, the use of the Neapolitan sixth chord on the word "mine" in measure 24 adds a climax to the textual meaning before the cadence of the last phrase. The regular, four-measure phrase patterns are consistent throughout the song except for the extension at the conclusion.

Specific Study Suggestions

The interpretation of this buoyant song is not difficult. The singer need only reflect in his bearing, his facial expression, and his tone quality the joy and sunshine of the text.

—Adopt a comfortable tempo.
—Carefully observe the melodic rhythm as an aid in projecting the mood of delight and peace in a momentary communing with nature, particularly in measures 3, 7, 15, 19, 23.
—In measure 14 be aware of the problem of singing on the first vowel of the diphthong until time to take a breath. Similar problems exist in the singing of the word "rise" in measure 18; "town" in measure 22; "mine" in measure 24; and "down" in measure 27.
—Avoid accenting second syllable of "quiet" in measure 13.
—Vocalize measures 24–25 on AH, making certain to attain the maximum stretch of the pharyngeal opening.

The Things Our Fathers Loved
(and the greatest of these was Liberty)

Charles Ives

Charles Ives, a composer who truly listened to "a different drummer," was born in Danbury, Connecticut, on October 20, 1874, and died in New York City on May 19, 1954. In this life span of eighty years Ives adventured into musical experiments far ahead of his time, such as polyrhythms, polytonality, dissonance, tone clusters, quarter tones, and aleatory music, in his effort to create a vital and living music related to life.

The single greatest influence on the musical life of Charles Ives was his father, George Ives. The senior Ives was a bandmaster in Danbury, Connecticut, who had an insatiable curiosity about sound. He loved the sounds of celebrations and patriotic occasions, as these had an "American" sound to him. More than these, however, he was fascinated by such ideas as tonal divisions and key associations, and carried out innumerable acoustical experiments that inspired his son in his future compositional experimentation.

Ives attended Yale University, where he studied composition with Horatio Parker and organ with Dudley Buck. Parker was unsympathetic to the creative experiments of his pupil and admonished him to keep to the regularly assigned work for his classes. He dutifully complied and did "write by the rules" while at the university.

Upon the completion of his formal studies in 1898, Ives made the serious decision to enter the world of business rather than the world of music in order to earn a living that would support a family. He well knew that the music he must write would not find a popular audience. His career in the insurance business was markedly successful. From his humble beginnings as a five-dollar-per-week actuarial clerk, he rose to a partnership in one of the most successful insurance agencies in New York.

During the years of his business life, which lasted until his health failed in his early forties, Ives poured out a large body of music. He worked unrelentingly during evening hours, weekends, and vacations, producing symphonies, violin sonatas, piano sonatas, two-string quartets, pieces for other instrumental combinations, choral works, and 114 songs. His music is extraordinarily diverse and the composer used daring and creative means to further his musical ideas even though he knew they would be unacceptable to the musicians of his day.

Diversity is the keyword in any description of the *114 Songs,* which appeared in a privately printed edition in 1922. In these songs, noted as among the most original of any produced in America, every mood and emotion can be found, from tender sentimentality to raucous humor. Also, every possible musical means is utilized in the interpretation of the texts, including extreme dissonances, polyrhythms, polymeters, bitonality, tone clusters, and atonality. The frequent use of musical quotations becomes a kind of musical reminiscence and reflects the composer's love of those nostalgic and uniquely American institutions such as the town band, camp meetings, and patriotic gatherings. The spirit and invention to be found in Ives's songs reflect the mind and heart of their creator and endow them with a directness of personal appeal for the listener.

Stylistic Features

"The Things Our Fathers Loved (and the greatest of these was Liberty)," to a text by the composer, was first published in 1922 in *114 Songs.* The text is a charming tribute to the "tunes" in each man's soul as inherited from his past. The melody incorporates snatches of six famous tunes nostalgic of an earlier time in American life. "Dixie" is found in measure 1; "My Old Kentucky Home" in measure 5; "On the Banks of the Wabash" in measure 6; "Nettleton" in measure 8; "The Battle Cry of Freedom" in measure

13; and "In the Sweet Bye and Bye" in measures 15–20. Ives refrains, however, from obvious allusions and disguises the old tunes with nontraditional harmonizations and rhythmic alterations.

Interesting touches of polytonality are found in measures 1–2, where the opening melodic figure is imitated in measure 2 as G#-F#-E, suggesting C Major plus E Major; and again in measure 3 as C#-B-A, suggesting F Major plus A Major. Another polytonal touch is found in the vocal line of measures 6–7. "On the Banks of the Wabash" is in G while the predominating harmonic sonorities are in a minor seventh in measure 6 and F triad plus sixth in measure 7.

In measure 13, the suggestion of "The Battle Cry of Freedom" is disguised by a slight rhythmic distortion. The effect is undoubtedly deliberate, as it occurs in connection with the words "Red, White, and Blue" and relates to the subtitle of the song, "and the greatest of these was Liberty."

The tonality of this song is not indicated. C Major is suggested in the opening three measures but this tonality is not confirmed by any later cadence or return. The unresolved ending of the song on a d# minor with added G# and B# is unsettling to the listener and could possibly be taken as a deliberate attempt to evoke the unsettled quality of the nostalgic mood.

Specific Study Suggestions

An imaginative "trip back in time" to a New England town of the late nineteenth century would be helpful to the performer in evoking the nostalgic mood of "The Things Our Fathers Loved." The first section of the song is quiet and introspective and should be sung as indicated, "slowly and sustained." However, as happy memories of town activities are revived in the second section of the song, beginning with measure 11, the mood brightens noticeably and the tempo quickens. A return to the meditative feeling of the opening phrases of the song appears in measure 19 and should be carefully delineated by the performer through tonal coloration as well as a slow and sustained tempo.

—In measure 6, exercise care to retain the vowels of each word as long as possible despite the rhythmic pattern of the dotted eighth note followed by a sixteenth. Any inclination to sing such a passage in a spasmodic manner would interfere with the legato demands and the clarity of text pronunciation.

—Beginning in measure 11 be aware of the importance of strong diaphragmatic support in order to meet the need for increased vitality of tone necessary to the urgency of the text.

—Study the melody independently of the accompaniment.

—Choral-speak the text following the melodic rhythm. Discuss the effect of melodic rhythm on mood depiction.

—Discuss text meanings and their effect on dynamics.

Two Little Flowers

(and dedicated to them)

rose' ___ passing fair; ___ The vi - o-let is ev-er dear, the
or - chid, ev - er ___ rare; There's lov - li - ness in wild flow'rs of ___
field or wide sa-van-nah, But fair-est, rar-est of them all are
E - dith and Su - san - na. ___

[1921]

Stylistic Features

"Two Little Flowers" was first published in 1922 in the *114 Songs*. It is said that the text of this song by Mrs. Ives was inspired by six-year-old Edith Ives and her playmate, Susanna Minturn. This endearing text reflects the glad love of parents for their greatest treasure.

The lyrical melodic line of a narrow range, which is characterized by scalewise passages and skips of thirds, fourths, and fifths, enhances the direct emotional appeal of this tender and loving text. However, any sentimentality is avoided by the unexpected rhythmic dislocations in measures 9, 13, and 17, which point up the words "in green," "passing fair," and "ever rare."

The gentle mood of the text is further supported by the light and deceptively simple arpeggiated accompaniment. Throughout the first ten measures of the song, the composer utilizes only one chord on a bass pedal of D. The distinctive aspect is the subtle rhythmic treatment of the arpeggiated accompaniment where an ostinato figure of seven eighth notes underlies the "square" four quarter patterns of the vocal line, thus providing a veiling effect. The unexpectedness of this treatment is another means adopted by the composer to avoid any semblance of sentimentality. Beginning in measure 15 to the end of the song, the composer enriches the harmonic content of the accompaniment through his use of a few color chords, including the whole tone chord in measures 15–18. The introduction is used as a codetta in the last three measures of the song.

Specific Study Suggestions

The gentle charm of this tender, lyrical expression of parental love presents few interpretive problems to the singer. "Two Little Flowers" should be sung with a disarming simplicity in every aspect. The legato flow of the melody should be uninterrupted throughout and the dynamic range limited in keeping with the graceful and delicate text meanings. Furthermore, few vocal problems are presented in this song. The lyric melodic line, which is largely scalewise in character, demands smooth, well-supported legato singing.

—Carefully observe the unusual setting of the text rhythms found in measures 9, 13, 17–18, as these represent a subtle device for expressive emphasis.

—Choral-speak text, utilizing melodic rhythm. Exercise particular care in observing rhythmic stresses and melodic syncopations in measures 9, 13, 16–18.

—Vocalize measures 13–18 on a neutral vowel while conducting, as an aid in attaining rhythmic accuracy.

—In measures 22–23 take particular care to modify the pronunciation of the vowel in "Fairest" toward the AYE, in order to insure good pitch in the melodic leap from b^1 to e^2.

—Note light-giving use of C# for "rarest," measure 23.

—Male voices may use alternate note in measure 24.

To Miss Maggie Teyte

MAY, THE MAIDEN

(Original Key)

SIDNEY LANIER   JOHN A. CARPENTER

John Alden Carpenter

John Alden Carpenter, a descendent of *Mayflower* pilgrim John Alden of Plymouth, was born in Park Ridge, Illinois, on February 28, 1876, and died in Chicago on April 26, 1951. As a youth he was given every educational opportunity open to one born into a family of wealth and culture. His first piano teacher was Amy Fay; later he studied piano and composition with W. C. E. Seeboeck. John Knowles Paine was his teacher at Harvard University, from which he graduated in 1897. While on a European trip he studied briefly with Edward Elgar in Rome before returning to Chicago, where he studied composition with Bernhard Ziehn for four years. Later in life the composer attributed much of his learning to this teacher.

Upon his graduation from Harvard, Carpenter became associated with his father's shipping firm and rose to the position of vice-president before retiring in 1936. Despite this lifetime of work in the marketplace, he managed to compose a large body of works in many forms and to achieve renown as a composer. He wrote two symphonies, choral works with orchestra, three ballets, five symphonic suites, chamber works, piano works, a violin sonata, and forty-three songs.

Carpenter was among the first Americans to incorporate the jazz idiom into his compositional work. In 1915 he employed ragtime rhythms in his concertino for piano and orchestra. And the two ballets "Krazy Kat" (1921) and "Skyscrapers" (1926) were also highly successful experiments in the popular style of the time. "Skyscrapers" was commissioned by the impresario Diaghilev, who was interested in a work depicting some aspects of American life. It was first produced at the Metropolitan Opera House in New York City in 1926. This work was highly praised at the time of its appearance and today is recognized for its historical significance as being the first large-scale work descriptive of American life.

Carpenter will undoubtedly be remembered as a composer of songs. His sensitivity to many moods and to the writings of diverse poets suggests the taste of a cultured man. "Water Colors," a cycle of Chinese tone poems translated by H. A. Giles, professor of Chinese at the University of Cambridge, and "Gitanjali," a cycle of the mystical texts of Rabindranath Tagore, are some of his best.

In the "Four Negro Songs" to texts by Langston Hughes, which appeared in 1930, the composer utilized jazz rhythms, a further reflection of his interest in a national music. He also set texts by such poets as Sassoon, Yeats, Lord Douglas, Oscar Wilde, Barnes, Blake, Stevenson, and Verlaine.

Stylistic Features

"May, the Maiden," to a text by Sidney Lanier, was composed in 1908 and appeared in a published version in 1912. The poetic atmosphere of the text is carried out in every aspect of the music by the composer in true nineteenth-century style. The refined line of the simple melody of a restricted range perfectly projects the romantic mood. The key of D Major is utilized in the first section of the song but in response to the textual quality of the B section the composer modulates into the dominant key. The use of descending chromaticisms in the piano accompaniment in measures 21–24 lends particular emphasis to the text. Also, the triplet figure in the melody in measures 18 and 19, as well as the dotted eighth note figure in measures 22–25, coloristically augments the urgency of the text.

In the piano interlude beginning with measure

28, before the return to the A section, the "dark" f# minor chord is employed leading into the word "night," followed by the dominant and tonic of the original key in measures 31–32. Thus there is a return to the gentle lyricism of the song's opening.

Specific Study Suggestions

"May, the Maiden" is an excellent study in legato singing. In the performance of this song the singer should represent through his facial expression and quiet bearing, as well as through a sustained tonal line, the tender lyric mood of the text. The slow one-beat-to-a-measure rhythmic swing, as indicated by the opening accompaniment figure of the dotted half note chord, and the largo indication are additional guides to the performer in carrying out the composer's intentions.

—Vocalize the melody of the A section on a neutral vowel, in order to fully sense the smoothness of the line.
—Avoid overweighting the voice in the short descending passages found in almost every measure of the song.
—Give careful attention to the necessary expansion of the rib cage on the intake of each breath and the subsequent very important support of the diaphragm throughout each phrase.
—Carefully observe rhythmic accuracy in triplets found in measures 18 and 19 on the words "sunken" and "violet."
—Note differing notational settings for "violet" found in measures 4, 5, 19, and 34.
—Be reminded to preserve the text mood as codetta is played.

An Old Song Re-sung

John Masefield*

Charles T. Griffes

*Words used by permission of The Macmillan Company, publishers of John Masefield's book; Copyright, 1912, by John Masefield.

bawl - ing at the rail - ing, Pi - ping thro' a sil - ver call that

had a chain of gold; The sum - mer wind was fail - ing and the

tall ship rolled. _____   I

Skins of musk - y yel - low wine, and silks in bales, Her

mer - ry men were cheer - ing, haul - ing on the brails.

I saw a ship a-sink - ing, a-

knock-ing off   the necks;_____ The

bro-ken glass was chink-ing as   she   sank   a-mong the   wrecks._____

Charles T. Griffes

Charles Griffes, "a name that deserves to be remembered," according to Aaron Copland, was born in Elmira, New York, on September 17, 1884, and died but thirty-five years later in New York City on April 8, 1920. His decidedly artistic gifts became evident very early. As a child he demonstrated a refined sensitivity to color in nature and to bird songs, which foretold his later preoccupation with color in sound.

The composer's first piano teacher was Miss Mary Broughton of Elmira, who recognized the extraordinary talents of her youthful student. She encouraged him and in 1903 made it financially possible for him to go to Berlin for study at the Stern Conservatory. After four years of study in Germany, Griffes returned to the United States in 1907 and faced the immediate problem of earning a living. He accepted a position as a music instructor at the Hackley School in Tarrytown, New York, where he was to remain for the remainder of his life.

In 1919 the recognition came to Griffes that established him as a leading composer of his day. "The Pleasure Dome of Kubla Khan" was performed by the Boston Symphony Orchestra conducted by Pierre Monteux; "The White Peacock," a tone poem for orchestra, was performed by the Philadelphia Orchestra with Leopold Stokowski conducting; the "Poem" for flute and orchestra was performed by George Barrère and the New York Symphony Orchestra with Walter Damrosch conducting.

The course of Griffes's stylistic development can be traced in his songwriting. The first set, "German Songs," written in 1909–10 to German texts, is indicative of the composer's German period; impressionistic influences can be detected in "Two Images" Op. 3; the exoticism of the orient is found in his "Five Poems of Ancient China and Japan" Op. 10; and the beginnings of new dissonances are to be found in "Three Poems by Fiona Macleod in Musical Settings" published shortly before his death.

Stylistic Features

"An Old Song Re-sung," to a John Masefield text, was composed in 1918 and published in 1920. The piano introduction sets the extravagantly boisterous mood of the text through the use of widely spaced block chords of open fourths and fifths within the framework of a dotted rhythm and triplets. Simple chords are used throughout the first strophe but occasionally they are altered chromatically to produce a special effect in response to the text, as in measures 7–9.

The piano interlude occurring before the second strophe again uses the pattern of the introduction. Although the obstreperous mood continues throughout this strophe, the welcome contrast of a lighter mood is provided by placing the left hand of the accompaniment in a higher octave.

The increasingly unrestrained textual meanings of the third strophe are emphasized by a reiteration of the widely spaced block chords of the introduction with the indication "più animato." In response to this exacerbation the composer briefly departs from the diatonicism of the first and second strophes and branches into consecutive chromatic chords in measures 30–36.

The postlude reflects the dénouement of the text in its mild texture and "piano" indication. A reminder of the earlier tumult is provided, however, in measure 41 with a recurrence of the opening theme of the melodic line.

Interest is created in the essentially simple melodic line of this vigorous, masculine song through the alternating use of a dotted-eighth rhythm as in measures 3–5 followed by four measures of a straight eighth-note, quarter-note plan.

In each of the three strophes some similarities in the melodic line may be found. The motivic pattern of measures 3–4 is repeated at the beginning of each strophe. However, in the third strophe strongly noticeable chromatic alterations appear, beginning with the downward leap of an augmented fourth in measure 31 in the setting of "spirit room." Further use of chromaticisms as well as an accelerated tempo is exceptionally effective in recreating the abandoned mood of the text.

Specific Study Suggestions

The successful interpretation of "An Old Song Re-sung" depends on a vigorous, vital tone quality, clarity of diction, and rhythmic precision. This song is essentially masculine in character but is a most useful study for all voices for the development of the ability to utilize maximum tonal support for an extended period and for the development of clarity of diction in the context of a syllabic setting.

The energetic rhythmic pattern found in the first strophe is repeated with slight variation in each succeeding strophe. This provides the clue to the need for a vital, robust interpretation. However, the singer has the problem of coordinating the necessary strong support of the breath with the need to clearly enunciate the syllabic setting of the text.

—Choral-speak the text, utilizing the melodic rhythm for awareness of rhythmic contrasts found in the melody. At the same time, give attention to flexibility of the lips for clarity of diction.

—Take full advantage of the opportunity for the expressive contrast of a legato passage with a "piano" indication found in measures 6–10 leading into the crescendo of measures 10–12.

—Practice slowly with piano accompaniment to develop precise rhythmic coordination, particularly in regard to such patterns found in measures 3–5 and 19–25.

—Exercise care in taking the necessary quick breaths as indicated in measures 4, 6, 8, 10, 15, 16, 18, 21, 28, 30, 33, 38. In each case it would be helpful to "rob" the note preceding the breath very slightly in order to attack the following note precisely in time.

—Be aware of the e minor scale found in measure 33 for pitch accuracy.

—Listen to accompaniment chords in measure 31 as an aid to pitch accuracy in the interval c^2–g^{b1}.

—Take note of the use of alliteration in measures 27–32 for a dramatic interpretive effect.

Wayfaring Stranger

Words and Music adapted from
The Original Sacred Harp

Arranged by
John Jacob Niles

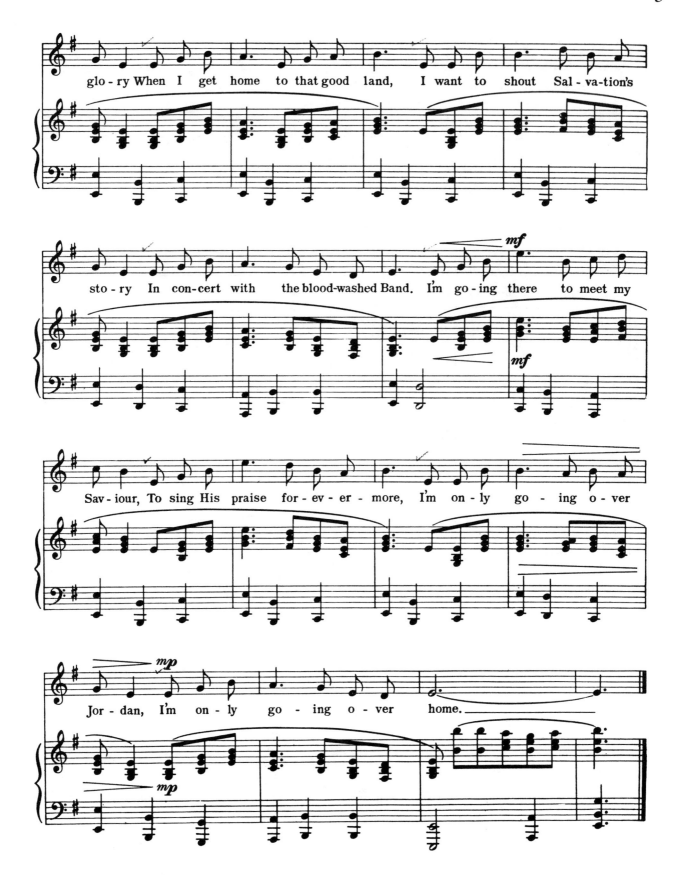

John Jacob Niles

A noted authority on American folk music of the southern Appalachians, John Jacob Niles was born in Louisville, Kentucky, on April 28, 1892. His early musical studies were at the Cincinnati Conservatory of Music. Later he studied at the University and Conservatory of Lyons and at the Schola Cantorum in Paris.

As a young man of twenty, Niles became interested in the music of the mountain people of the southern Appalachian region of the United States, who stem from seventeenth-century England. Although he wished to develop interesting material for his own performance use, he also had a true awareness of the worth of this music and the importance of preserving this heritage. Niles had the conviction that every individual has the right to experience his or her "roots" through the folk music of his or her past.

Niles persisted in his folk song collecting for over fifty years. His lifelong adventure in pursuit of tunes brought him not only untold satisfactions but also an appreciation of Elizabethan balladry and its imperishability. He believed that Elizabethan balladry was the basis of a truly Anglo-American musical idiom that should, at all costs, be preserved.

Stylistic Features

Everyman's search for "home," depicted in the text of "Wayfaring Stranger," is of universal appeal. According to Niles, the text and tune are of unknown origin. He took the version used in this arrangement from an all-day "singing" in a church at Shootin' Creek, North Carolina.

Simplicity is the keynote in this strophic setting. The aeolian melody, typical of the folk genre with its limited range and characteristic descending minor third interval, is ideally suited to the doleful text.

The melody is outlined throughout by the right hand of the accompaniment. The block chords utilized in strophes one and three are altered to a single line for the second strophe.

The bass line of the accompaniment in the first strophe is composed, for the most part, of a three-note ostinato figure, as in measures 6–10 and 15–17. The same figure reappears in the third strophe but in octaves, beginning at measure 44.

Specific Study Suggestions

The successful interpretation of "Wayfaring Stranger" is dependent upon a quietly intense projection of the thoughtful text and, at the same time, the retention of a simple and unaffected folk song style. It is important to maintain a lovely legato flow throughout, despite the difficulty presented by the setting of a separate syllable on every note of the melody.

The need for subtle variety in dynamic shadings in such a repetitive melody is a second problem in the study of this song. The significance of the textual meanings should be the guide to the necessary colorations. The gradually increasing intensity of each succeeding strophe is a clear indication of the need to enrich the vocal color, as in measures 33–37 and again in measures 47–54.

—Vocalize the melody on a neutral vowel, in order to become keenly aware of the smooth and connected aspect of the line.
—Apply the text to the vocal line, striving to maintain the sense of singing on the vowels.
—Avoid any temptation to force the voice when responding to increasing textual intensity.
—Be conscious of strengthening diaphragm support when responding to textual intensity.

Fog

Medium Voice

* Words by
Carl Sandburg

Music by
ROY HARRIS

* From CHICAGO POEMS by Carl Sandburg, Copyright 1916 by Henry Holt and Company. Copyright 1943 by Carl Sandburg.

Roy Harris

Roy Harris was born of pioneer parents in a log cabin in Lincoln County, Oklahoma, on February 12, 1898, the anniversary of Abraham Lincoln's birth. The event was an auspicious happening in time and place for the man who was to create, according to Aaron Copland, music "vital in today's American scene." Musically, his youth was uneventful. The family migrated to a farm in Covina, California, in 1903 and there his mother taught him the rudiments of the piano. After service in the heavy artillery during World War I, he entered the University of California but remained for only one year. It was not until Harris was twenty-four years old, after drifting from place to place and from job to job, that he came to a final decision that music was to be his life work.

The composer's first formal study of theory and composition was with Arthur Farwell; he studied orchestration with Modest Altschuler. Farwell recognized the genius of his student and encouraged him to submit one of his compositions, the "Andante for Orchestra," to the Eastman School of Music's 1926 Festival of American Music. The piece was performed, not only in Rochester, New York, at the Eastman School, but also at the Hollywood Bowl and in New York at the Lewisohn Stadium concerts that same year. Study in Paris, under the tutelage of Nadia Boulanger, followed. Guggenheim Fellowships in 1927 and 1928 enabled Harris to remain in Paris until 1929.

In his long and productive career after returning to the United States in 1929, until his death in Santa Monica, California, in 1979, Roy Harris composed works in almost every form except opera. The large forms predominate in the catalogue and include twelve symphonies, three ballets, chamber works for a wide variety of instrumental combinations, choral and vocal works, and piano works. The composer's approach to music was distinctly individual and he consciously searched for an expression that is recognizably American in character. He believed that the American rhythmic impulses are unique and that this sensibility is responsible for different melodic and form values. Also he recognized that American composers, in their search for an American idiom, were breaking with tradition in varying ways. In their search for newness and in their aversion to finality, Americans began experimenting with the avoidance of definite cadences. They also began experimenting in the uses of modal harmony in a search for exoticism and in an effort to escape the more conventional major and minor scales.

Stylistic Features

This setting of "Fog," one of the best-known and most-anthologized poems of Carl Sandburg, was composed in 1948. The renowned descriptive text of a natural phenomenon is set in every detail with thoughtful care for its amorphous, hazy quality. The mood is set in the four measure introduction with a deep ominous pedal tone on a d^b that is maintained throughout the song except in measures 15 and 22. This device, combined with the polychordal harmonic style, creates a rich but subtle texture entirely suited to the vaporous and impressionistic mood. The apparent key of D^b minor (sometimes Major) has a polytonal overlay of d minor. The vocal line expresses a strong d minor tonality at the opening, and especially in measures 12–15.

The harmonic style is an excellent illustration of the application of Harris's theory of sonorities based on superimposed triads (polychords). For example, in measure 5 (a d minor triad over the D^b Major in the lower parts) and in measure 8, a b minor seventh chord sounding over the B Major below, the sonorities dramatize the nebulous and pervasive aspect of the poetic meanings.

The vocal line is suitably slow-moving throughout. In the introduction a significant melodic motif, a–a♭, is utilized to interpret the opening line of the song, "the fog comes," as well as the last line, "then moves on." Interestingly, this interval is reiterated throughout the song in the accompaniment, providing a unifying element.

Specific Study Suggestions

"Fog" is an excellent study in mood projection by means of pure legato singing. The vocal aspect of the song is very short but within each brief phrase the interpreter has the opportunity to create a unique atmosphere. Even though the dynamic level remains low throughout, the tone must be well-supported at all times. It is well to remember that soft singing demands the same care in tonal support as that required for a fuller tone. Also, careful enunciation of the text is most important in this quiet song.

—In measure 6 give attention to an expressive emphasis on the word "comes." The effect would be furthered by careful attention to the enunciation of the consonants in the word.

—Sing the long phrase beginning with measure 13 smoothly and without any crescendo, in keeping with the mysterious mood.

—In measure 13 avoid stress on the "ng" ending of the word "looking." Rather, go directly from the vowel in the word ending to the vowel in "over" in measure 14. With careful attention to such a small detail the arch of the melodic line will be uninterrupted and the mood thus continuously sustained.

—Negotiate the octave leap in measure 20 without undue weight on the d^1.

—Precisely observe the melodic rests found in measures 15–18 and 20, but avoid disrupting the mood by audibility of breath intake. Think of singing "through the rests."

—In measure 21 a pure "oo" vowel in the word "moves" is extremely important as the resultant tonal color would effectively carry out the chimerical textual meanings.

—Be aware of meter changes to and from 4/4 to 5/4 found throughout the song.

—Exercise care concerning pitch accuracy on the voice entrance in measure 5 on d^1 against the d♭ in the bass.

—Listen closely to accompaniment in measure 21 as an aid in pitch accuracy on descending thirds.

—Experiment with the application of a "straight tone" color for depiction of veiling effect of fog. Male voices could utilize a pure head voice for this effect.

To Frances Crane Lillie

THE DIVINE SHIP

Walt Whitman

ERNST BACON

Ernst Bacon

An outstanding and outspoken exponent of the "American" in all aspects of America's musical life, Ernst Bacon was born in Chicago on May 26, 1898. Bacon's early musical education was in Chicago. After taking the M.A. degree at the University of Chicago, he went to Vienna for further studies in piano, conducting, and composition. Upon returning to the United States, he did advanced work with Ernest Bloch in composition and with Eugene Goossens in conducting at the Eastman School of Music. Bacon enjoyed a distinguished teaching career in various posts and in 1945 became director of the School of Music of Syracuse University in upstate New York.

In his early work as a composer ("Ten Songs," published in 1928) Bacon followed the example of an earlier generation in using German texts set in the German romantic style. However, in the 1940s Bacon wrote his own Declaration of Independence in his famous and much-quoted article, "Toward a Musical Home Rule," in which he pledged himself to develop his musical materials as an American rather than as the student of a European tradition. He said that Americans should be independent in art, foregoing all imitation of the older European tradition. At all costs, even that of failure, originality must be fostered, he believed.

After the time of that article, Bacon's large output manifested his new point of view. He became interested in national American subjects as well as the folk song. This preoccupation with Americana was reflected in his two folk operas and his orchestral suites. In his more than two hundred songs, he utilized numerous American folk songs in his thematic material as well as texts by American poets in his settings.

Stylistic Features

"The Divine Ship," set to a text by the American poet Walt Whitman, was published in a set entitled "Quiet Airs" in 1952. The text is a deeply philosophical reflection on human destiny, which the composer points up in every detail of this distinguished song. The chorale-like melodic line of a narrow range, characterized by limited skips of thirds, fourths and fifths, is designed to be interpreted in a "stately" manner. The accompaniment adds to the dignity of the song by a sustained chordal pattern of the left hand depicting the strong supporting pillars, which suggest the immutability of the textual meaning. The flowing contrapuntal melody of the right hand might suggest the flow of life toward its end. The harmonization is modal with accidentals, further evoking the mystical meanings of the text. The form of this short through-composed song is one part with phrase groups as in a chorale. There is no introduction or postlude.

Specific Study Suggestions

The dignity of the Whitman text is the key to the interpretation of "The Divine Ship." The sustained line of the melody should be sung with a smooth legato and fully supported tone. The intensity of the last phrase, "Are bound to the same destination," must be maintained despite the descending pattern of the melodic line. Avoidance of rubato is also to be recommended in the performance of this song in order to further preserve the strength of the textual meaning.

—Rhythmically intone the text in order to become fully aware of the depth of meaning inherent in the text.

—Be aware of moving from vowel to vowel in singing the text without permitting the consonants to interfere with the clarity of the vowels. Particular stresses should be avoided as the composer treats each syllable of the text equally.

—Keep the vowels stable and undistorted. This is important when required to sustain the vowel four, six, or eight beats as in measures 4, 11, 17, 25, and 26.

—Vocalize each phrase separately on a neutral vowel such as OO or AH before using the text, in order to develop a sense of tonal flow in this slow-moving song.

—Breath intake must be inaudible and in no way impede the tonal flow should it be necessary to take a breath more frequently than at the ends of phrases. This song offers an opportunity for practice in a quick spread of the rib cage without any lifting of the chest for the achievement of a rapid, full, and, at the same time, inaudible breath.

—Note stress marks found over each note in measures 1–4, followed by the indication "simile," which points up the composer's strong feeling that each tone of the melodic line is of equal importance and should receive equal sustained treatment.

LOVE'S SECRET

(William Blake)

OTTO LUENING

vis - ib - ly.

I— told my love, I told my love, I told her all my

heart, Trem-bling, cold, in ghast-ly fears   Ah! she did de-

part!

Otto Luening

Otto Luening, a composer who has had an unusual influence on the direction of twentieth-century music, was born in Milwaukee, Wisconsin, on June 15, 1900. When he was twelve years of age his parents enrolled him in the Royal Academy of Music in Munich and in 1917 he went to the Municipal Conservatory in Zurich. Privately he worked with Ferruccio Busoni, who exerted a strong influence on his future thinking in creative music. His years as professor of music at Columbia University were extraordinarily productive. A large catalogue of music in a wide variety of styles, including theatre works, large orchestral works, chamber works, choral works, and numerous songs, has been produced. His songs represent one-third of his creative output. His opera "Evangeline," composed to his own libretto and produced at Columbia University in 1948, won the David Bispham medal.

Together with Vladimir Ussachevsky, a colleague at Columbia, Luening began working in tape-music composition in the late 1940s and early 1950s. By the fall of 1952, the two composers had produced enough compositions in this medium to present the first concert of tape music at the Museum of Modern Art in New York. Luening continued his experiments in the new medium, basing his work on solo flute sounds, and produced "Invention and Fantasy in Space," "Low Speed," and "Invention." In 1954 Luening and Ussachevsky produced on commission by the Louisville Symphony Orchestra "Rhapsodic Variations." The performance on March 20, 1954 was the first public performance of a work for tape recorder and symphony orchestra.

In 1959, aided by a Rockefeller Foundation Grant, Luening and Ussachevsky, together with Milton Babbitt and Roger Sessions of Princeton University, established the Columbia-Princeton Electronic Music Center at Columbia University. A synthesizer was developed by the Radio Corporation of America, which made it possible to develop totally organized music with precise control. In ruminating on these developments Luening has expressed certain doubts concerning the "totally planned spontaneity" of the new medium. Nevertheless, important works in the medium of electronic music have come from the Center. Furthermore, the Center has been active in advisement on the establishment of other centers throughout the United States.

Stylistic Features

"Love's Secret," by Luening, utilizes simple but subtle means to point up the distinctive qualities of the Blake text. The accompaniment opens with a major tonality, which lends a seeming carefree and folklike mood. The tonality rapidly changes to the minor upon the introduction of the text presaging the unhappiness and cynicism inherent in the poetry.

The motivic pattern of the first two measures of the introduction is used in the vocal line at the opening of each strophe, as in measures 5–6; 17–18; 29–30. This repetitive feature not only provides a unifying factor but also serves as an additional folklike element. The gentle, rhythmically unsophisticated melody is characterized by modest skips within a limited range. Textual meanings are frequently enhanced by the melodic direction. This factor is especially apparent in measures 11–12 in outlining the words "silently, invisibly"; in measures 23–24 to color "Ah! she did depart!"; and similarly in measures 35–36, "He took her with a sigh."

The deceptive cadence idea at measures 3–4 is

carried out at the end of each strophe of the song (measures 16 and 27–28). This may be interpreted as another means of pointing up the "deceptiveness" of the lover. The postlude echoes the unifying motivic material introduced in the first two measures of the song, this time in C Major. The prolonged final chord on C Major could be interpreted as a reiteration of the "sigh" of the cynical lover.

Specific Study Suggestions

This folklike setting of William Blake's text presents few vocal problems to the interpreter. The descriptive nature of the poetry, however, demands the full play of the singer's imagination in order to fulfill the interpretive needs. Also, the rolled chords employed throughout in the accompaniment allow some degree of rhythmic freedom as well as facilitating the conception.

—Discuss text meanings and their relevance in developing the interpretation.
—Note the careful interpretive markings of the composer throughout: "rit. poco" in measure 11;

"hesitate" in measures 12, 16, 28; "slower" in measures 21, 27, 33; "slow up" in measure 35.
—Observe meter changes to and from 3/2 to ¢ found throughout the song as a mnemonic aid.
—Observe pauses indicated in measures 11, 30, 33, 34 for expressive purposes.
—Be reminded to observe good posture, including full diaphragmatic support of the tone, throughout, despite the rubato inherent to the interpretation.
—Give particular attention to the melodic leaps found in measures 9–10, 22–23, and 34–35. In each case it is important that the singer be aware of the tonal flow from vowel to vowel without permitting interference from the consonants. In each case an effective interpretation of the text demands the utmost purity of the vowels.
—In measures 10–11 youthful contraltos and basses may substitute a c^2 on the word "move," remaining on c^2 for the first syllable of "Silently" and resolving to b^{b1} for the remaining two syllables of the word.
—Note variations in accompaniment figure for each strophe as an aid in developing interpretive coloration.

II
HEART

B.B. 26

B.B. 26

Jean Berger

Jean Berger was born in Hamm, Germany, on September 27, 1901. He studied musicology in Heidelberg, earning the Ph.D. degree in 1931. For the next eight years he studied composition in Paris under Louis Aubert and was professionally active as a choral conductor. After a two-year period in Rio de Janeiro, where he coached French opera, Berger settled in New York in 1941. He became a citizen of the United States in 1943. In 1948 Berger joined the faculty of Middlebury College, where he served until 1959, when he went to the University of Illinois at Urbana. From 1961 to 1968 he was on the faculty of the University of Colorado.

As a composer, Jean Berger is especially interested in the voice, although he has composed in many forms, including orchestral works and chamber music. More than two hundred of his choral works are in print, many of which are recognized as standard works in the repertoire by choruses throughout North America and Europe. Sacred works predominate the catalogue, although there is a significant number of secular compositions. His works are noted for their lyricism as well as for their singability.

Stylistic Features

"Heart," by Jean Berger, was composed in 1951 and is the second song in a cycle entitled *Four Songs* to texts by Langston Hughes. "Heart" is concerned with the tragedy of Pierrot the clown, who forever entertains others but cannot find love for himself.

The simple and sustained melody is limited in range but is inherently interesting due to subtle rhythmic variation, key changes, and meter changes. The hemiola rhythm used in measure 9 lends increased meaning to the single word "wayside."

Again in measure 23 the same hemiola rhythm is used to point up "public wall."

The doleful mood is established in the introduction by means of the minor key and the "emptiness" of the widely spaced open chords. The left hand of the accompaniment has a pedal-like pattern in measures 1–12. An abrupt meter and key change in measure 13 emphasizes the change in the text from a description of Pierrot's plight to his actual plea to the passerby. A further meter and key change in measure 17, as well as a "più mosso" indication, illuminates the descriptive text.

The accompaniment pattern of the song's opening returns in measures 26–33, but, this time, is repeated twice. The song ends simply and quietly with the melody outlining the minor chord in a descending pattern while the accompaniment outlines a brief ascending pattern in thirds and fourths, with a "ppp" indication that provides a vivid picture of the question asked: "Where his heart is Today."

Specific Study Suggestions

The effective interpretation of this lovely song depends to a great extent on the imagination of the interpreter. Consequently, it is important that text meanings be clearly understood in order that the singer be enabled to subtly dramatize the text by expressive means as well as vocal means.

—Discuss text meanings for clear understanding. It would be helpful to view a print or slide of a clown by such outstanding artists as Picasso or Roualt for a deepening awareness.
—Choral-speak the text utilizing the melodic rhythm. Conducting during this activity will aid in the development of rhythmic precision in all cases of meter change as well as in the occasional

syncopation. This activity is also extremely useful for accuracy in memorization.

—Vocalize on a neutral vowel measures 5–11 for development of legato. Following vocalization, sing the text while striving to attain the legato ease

of the vocalization.

—Use care to bring out the contrasts offered by the text.

—Use great care for clarity of diction. It is important to "tell the story."

To Sophie Sargent

The Lamb

William Blake

Theodore Chanler

Theodore Chanler

Theodore Chanler was born in Newport, Rhode Island, on April 29, 1902 and died in Boston on July 7, 1961. His early musical education was in Boston, under the direction of Hans Ebell in piano and Arthur Shepherd in composition. In 1920 he came under the influence of Ernest Bloch and, along with other gifted young composers, went to the newly founded Cleveland Institute of Music to be with him. In 1923 he went to England to study at Oxford University and two years later went to Paris to study with Nadia Boulanger. In 1933 he returned to the United States.

Chanler attained distinction not only as a composer but also as a music critic and writer on musical subjects. As a regular contributor to the publication *Modern Music* until its demise, his articles covered a wide range of thoughtful studies on all aspects of the art of music.

Chanler composed primarily in the small forms, although he did write a ballet, a violin sonata, a Mass for two female voices and organ, piano works, and a chamber opera. He was most distinguished for his lyrical atmospheric songs, which were widely praised upon their appearance. The songs reflected his avowed interest in the music of Fauré and, as Robert Tangeman wrote in *Modern Music,* displayed an integrated maturity of style, bringing a new beauty into American music.

Stylistic Features

"The Lamb," to a text by William Blake, was published in 1946. This childlike and gentle strophic song is an outstanding example of Chanler's song writing. Every aspect of the composition reflects the mystical Blake text concerning the Lamb of God who "takest away the sins of the world." The short introduction sets the mood with its contrapuntal texture. The use of the melodic minor in this introductory phrase, with the slight touch of the aeolian mode in the base line of measure 2, helps to establish the ineffability of the atmosphere.

The rhythmic speech pattern of the melody mirrors the text in every detail of its refinement and lyricism. Also, symbolism can be discerned in the careful use of melodic direction. For the rhetorical question "who made thee?" in measure 3 the melody ascends, whereas the melodic descent for the same text in measure 4 might be interpreted as a positive melodic answer. A similar expressive device is used in measures 9 and 10. The stepwise ascent to the third of the melody for the words "tender voice" and the arpeggiated ascent to the fifth for "vales rejoice" are particularly noteworthy.

The simplicity of the piano accompaniment supports the abstruse textual meanings throughout. An implied uncertainty through the deceptive progression of V–VI at the little cadence in measure 4 colors and emphasizes the text "who made thee?" Also, the unexpected Neapolitan chord in measure 7 colors the beautiful line "Gave thee clothing of delight." The reiteration of the first line of the text found in measures 11 and 12 now appears in the parallel major key. This time the wondering rhetorical question has found its answer in the positive major key. All these effects reappear in the second strophe.

Specific Study Suggestions

The loveliness and wonder of the Blake text must be carefully delineated by the interpreter of "The Lamb." It is important to enunciate carefully and, at the same time, to maintain a quiet lyric tone in keeping with the tranquility of the poetry.

The song is an especially good study for two important problems: firstly, for the development of a capability in taking rapid, inaudible breaths. for at no point in either stanza does the composer allow an actual rest, which would enable the singer to take a long breath; secondly, for singing with a smooth legato line without any suggestion of slurring, in order to avoid sentimentalizing the interpretation.

—Work to develop a refined legato despite the syllabic setting, in order to maintain the delicacy of the text meanings.

—Work for clarity of diction while maintaining the legato flow.

—Have a consciousness of singing through the breath so as to avoid any interruption of the reflective mood.

—Place the hands about the lower rib cage, the fingers pointed toward the spine, while directing the attention to a quick spread of the ribs for the breath intake.

—Negotiate the leap of the fifth in measures 3, 4, 9, and 10 with a sense of a rapid and smooth flow from vowel to vowel. Simultaneously, direct careful attention to the maintenance of good tonal support.

—Note the use of the parallel key of F Major in the melody, measures 9–12 and 21–24, as a subtle, expressive means of pointing up text meanings.

—Note the Picardy third in the final cadence of each strophe, measures 12 and 24, as a musical depiction of the rhetorical question of the text.

Sound the Flute!

William Blake

Celius Dougherty

Celius Dougherty

Celius Dougherty, who was to make a brilliant reputation as an accompanist as well as a composer, was born in Glenwood, Minnesota, on May 27, 1902. Upon the completion of his undergraduate studies at the University of Minnesota, where he studied piano and composition with Donald Ferguson, he was accepted as a scholarship student at the Juilliard School of Music. Rubin Goldmark was his composition teacher and he studied piano under Josef Lhévinne.

For many years Celius Dougherty traveled extensively as accompanist to numerous world-famous singers. Also, during those years he composed many songs that were introduced to the public by such artists as Gladys Swarthout, Blanche Thebom, Roland Hayes, and Bidú Sayão. Since retiring from his work as an accompanist, Celius Dougherty has continued to write for the voice as well as to fulfill many commissions for such well-known artists as Thomas Stewart and Evelyn Lear, James King and Phyllis Curtin. In a letter to the author, Mr. Dougherty speaks of his feeling for the vocal instrument: "I believe I always hear the voice singing—I like what it can do, more than any other instrument maybe, and I try to find texts that will provide it with melodic line."

Stylistic Features

"Sound the Flute," to a text by William Blake, is a charming and bright celebration of welcome to the New Year. Every aspect of the strophic setting carries out the gayety of the mood. The melody, limited to a sixth in range, is buoyant and lilting due to the ingenious melodic rhythm.

The top line of the accompaniment in section A follows the vocal line, but an octave above, and utilizes staccato chords of thirds and fourths, which provide a light and airy texture in keeping with the mood of the text. The left hand of the accompaniment in the first strophe, also in the treble clef, is very light, never intruding on the delicate mood.

In the second strophe the left hand accompaniment of the first strophe is repeated but the composer provides variation to the repetitive nature of the melodic line and the left hand of the accompaniment by means of slight changes in the rhythmic patterns of the treble line. Further variation is provided in the last section of the song by lowering both the right and the left hands of the accompaniment one octave. The triple piano indication as well as the light texture prevents any possibility of detracting from the cheerful mood by this device.

Specific Study Suggestions

The interpretation of "Sound the Flute" depends on the ability of the performer to project joyousness in facial expression as well as in tone quality, in response to the happiness of the text. This song is an excellent study for clarity of diction.

—At first, utilize a moderate tempo when practicing, in order to insure the rhythmic precision of the melodic line.
—Carefully observe the dotted eighth notes of the melody as found in measures 3, 7, 10, 11, etc.
—Choral-speak the text, utilizing the melodic

rhythm for the development of precision as well as for lip and tongue action.

—Give particular attention to the problem of clear diction without jaw involvement.

—Note the meter changes as in measures 4, 8, etc., and carefully observe the indicated phrasing as an aid to interpretation.

—Give careful attention to the need for dynamic variation from strophe to strophe for interpretive purposes.

LAZY AFTERNOON
(from "Ozark Set")

Words by
LEO PARIS

Music by
ELIE SIEGMEISTER

Oliverea. 1943

Elie Siegmeister

Elie Siegmeister was born in New York City on January 15, 1909. He studied composition with Seth Bingham at Columbia University and worked privately with Wallingford Riegger. Upon graduation from Columbia in 1927 he went to Paris to study with Nadia Boulanger and remained in Paris for the next five years. It was in Paris that he felt the need to find an American expression in music, an expression that could find a response in a wide cross-section of the people.

Upon his return to the United States, Siegmeister became interested in the folk music of America. He traveled extensively throughout the country in order to hear folk music and to notate what he heard. The subject matter of his early works reflected this nationalistic interest, with such titles as *American Holiday, Ozark Set, Prairie Legend, Wilderness Road* and *Western Suite*.

In the ensuing years Elie Siegmeister has built a multifaceted career as an educator and writer as well as a composer. Since 1949 he has been on the faculty of Hofstra University as professor of music as well as composer-in-residence. His *Treasury of American Song,* edited in collaboration with Olin Downes (1943), was an important outcome of his folk music research. Other writings include *The Music Lover's Handbook* (1943), *Invitation to Music* (1959), *Harmony and Melody,* 2 vols. (1965), and *The New Music Lover's Handbook* (1971). The large catalogue of works includes operas, three symphonies and other orchestral works, piano music, chamber music, and many songs. Also, he has composed for the theatre and for films.

Stylistic Features

"Lazy Afternoon" from *Ozark Set,* to a text by Leo Paris, was composed by Elie Siegmeister in 1957. The indolent mood of a summer afternoon in the country, with all desire for achievement left far behind, is supported in all respects by the setting. The folklike repetitive melody with its characteristic descending interval at the end of each phrase emphasizes the aimless character of the text meanings.

The simple syncopated accompaniment lends further support to the idle mood of the song. In the second strophe the composer provides new interest by utilizing the melodic line in the right hand of the accompaniment but one octave higher than the vocal line and by using broken chords in the left hand. In the third strophe the composer reverts to the syncopated, chordal structure of the first strophe. The lightness of the harmonic texture throughout and the repetitive syncopated rhythmic swing of the accompaniment underline the repetitive melody of this charming evocation of a summer day in the country.

Specific Study Suggestions

This folklike melody should be sung with the utmost simplicity throughout for an effective interpretation. A light but well-supported tone should be used in keeping with the casual mood. However, the melodic rhythm should be precisely correct, as its syncopated character enhances the evocation of the lazy mood.

—Conduct a slow two to a measure in order to sense the leisurely swing of the rhythm while choral-speaking the text within the framework of the melodic rhythm.

—Note the composer's use of syncopation for expressive purposes as in measures 3 and 5, 11 and 13, etc.

—Do not permit the casual mood to affect intonation at any point, especially on the descending interval found at the end of each phrase.

—Exercise care in the use of clear diction throughout. Be reminded to "sing on the vowels."

To Mme. Povla Frijsh

The Pasture

Robert Frost*

Charles Naginski

clean   the pas - ture   spring;

I'll on-ly stop to rake the leaves a - way   (And

*From "Collected Poems" by Robert Frost. By permission of Henry Holt and Company, Publishers.

wait   to watch the   wa - ter clear,_____ I   may):

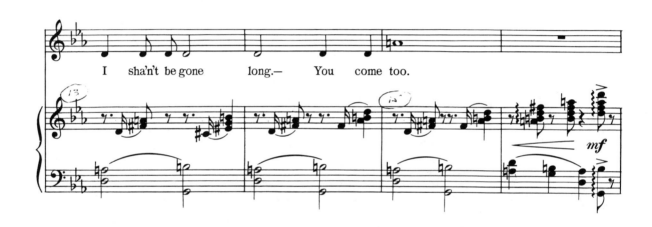

I   sha'n't be gone   long.— You   come too.

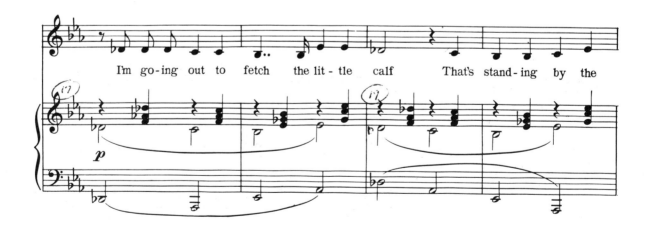

I'm go-ing out to fetch   the lit - tle calf   That's stand-ing by the

Charles Naginski

Charles Naginski was born in Cairo, Egypt, on May 29, 1909. His premature death by drowning in Lenox, Massachusetts, on August 4, 1940 cut short a remarkably promising career as a composer. The marked talent for composition that Naginski evidenced at a very early age was recognized by his father, his first piano teacher. From 1928 to 1933 Naginski held a fellowship at the Juilliard Graduate School as a pupil of Rubin Goldmark. Later he studied at the American Academy in Rome, winning the American Prix de Rome in 1938.

The catalogue of his works includes an orchestral suite (1931); two string quartets (1933); an orchestral poem (1936); Sinfonietta (1937); Three Movements for chamber orchestra (1937); The Minotaur, ballet for orchestra (1938); Nocturne and Pantomime (1938); Five Pieces from a Children's Suite (Boston, 1940); and songs.

The songs, although limited in number, are of high quality and deserve a wide public.

Stylistic Features

"The Pasture," to a text by Robert Frost, was published in 1949. The two-measure introduction sets the folklike, "walking" mood of the text by means of the double dotted figure in the left hand of the accompaniment as well as the rhythmic pattern of the right hand. Unobtrusive dissonances are utilized in the first part of the two-part song to enhance the diatonic melodic line.

The short one-measure interlude leading into the second section provides an interesting key alteration leading into D^b Major in measure 17. The mood of the first section prevails in the second but this time the composer provides interesting variety by means of a change in the rhythmic pattern of the accompaniment.

Melodic material is in keeping with the simplicity of the text throughout. In the first section the melody essentially outlines the tonic chord until measure 13. In measure 14 the composer begins the transition to a new key in measure 17. Further key changes in the second section provide quiet interest, with a final return to the original E^b Major (of the song's opening) in measure 28.

Specific Study Suggestions

This charming song should be sung quietly and unaffectedly in keeping with the atmosphere of this tranquil moment in the country. Few vocal problems present themselves in this folklike song. It is important, however, that the performer be imaginative in fulfilling the interpretive demands of the text.

—Clear diction is especially important despite the "piano" indication to tell the story of the text.
—Be reminded to provide good tonal support despite the quietude of the mood. Soft singing demands the same diaphragmatic support as does forte singing.
—Use care in singing the melodic leaps, as in measures 3–4 and throughout, for pitch accuracy. Vocalize such passages on "AH" in order to achieve a sense of tonal line. Following this exercise, utilize the text, making an effort to attain the same tonal line.
—Use care to vary the tone quality in measures 9–12 in order to set off the parenthetical text.
—In measure 25 follow the detached indication for interpretive effect.

to Sara

Sure on this shining night

James Agee*

Samuel Barber, Op. 13, No. 3
Original Key

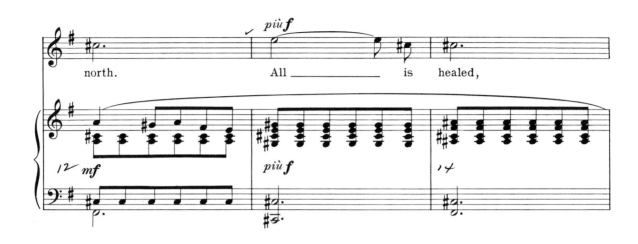

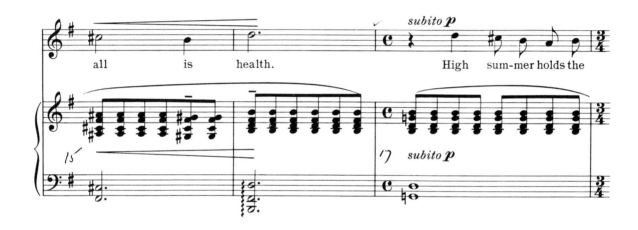

Samuel Barber

Samuel Barber, one of America's most important twentieth-century composers, was born in West Chester, Pennsylvania, on March 9, 1910. As a child he demonstrated a pronounced talent for composition. His aunt was the celebrated contralto Louise Homer. Perhaps it was this influence that prompted him at age ten to attempt writing an opera.

Barber was a charter student at the Curtis Institute of Music in Philadelphia, which he entered at thirteen. He graduated from the Curtis in 1932. Barber won a number of important awards, which made it possible for him to devote his entire time to composition. The Bearns prize in 1928 enabled him to go abroad for study and travel. Later important prizes included the American Prix de Rome in 1935 and two Pulitzer prizes for music in 1935 and 1936.

Barber has composed in all the large forms as well as songs. Two symphonies, two operas, choral works, concerti, and chamber works are all included in an impressive catalogue, as well as the songs. Being a singer himself meant that the composer brought to this work a thorough understanding of the vocal instrument and its interpretive powers. A wide gamut of emotion can be found in the songs, from the sweet lyricism of "The Daisies" to the strength and power of "Bessie Bobtail" and "I hear an army." "The Hermit Songs," which appeared in 1952, have been awarded the highest critical acclaim. In these songs Barber utilizes many twentieth-century techniques such as disjointed vocal lines, metric irregularity, and harmonic complexity, but always retains tonality.

Stylistic Features

"Sure on this shining night," the third song of Op. 13, to a text by James Agee, was composed in 1938.

The lyricism of the introspective text is carried out in every aspect of this song in ternary form. In the first section, measures 1–9, the voice initiates the theme in measure 2. In canonic style the right hand of the piano accompaniment reiterates the theme, beginning in measure 3 a third higher. The melodic line "sings" uninterruptedly from beginning to end either in the voice part or in the accompaniment. At such infrequent intervals when rests are indicated for the voice, as in measures 4 and 10, the canonic character of the accompaniment provides an uninterrupted continuation of the melodic line. Upon the return to the A section of the song at measure 21, the composer reverses the procedure of measures 2–3. He then initiates the theme in the piano and allows the voice to imitate the theme a third higher.

The middle section of the song presents a brief excursion into the key of b minor in measure 10. The climax of this section in measure 14, with the words, "All is healed," is emphasized by the "joyful" F# Major chord (dominant of b minor). A similar bright effect is created by the use of the major key in measures 17–20 after the minor.

Specific Study Suggestions

The beauty and dignity of this reflective text are a clear indication to the singer for the interpretation of "Sure on this shining night." The means employed by the composer in the conception of his intentions, including the moderate tempo indication, the major key, and the pure lyricism of the almost scalewise melodic line, are further guides to a successful realization. This song presents a good study in legato singing.

—Sing the opening statement with a well-supported tone.

—Consciously sing from vowel to vowel, not permitting the slightest interference in the tonal line from the consonants.

—In measure 10 careful attention should be given to the purity of the vowel in the word "late." This care will enable the singer to bring the necessary intensity to the interpretation at this point, leading into the climax of the song on the word "health" in measure 16.

—Eliminate all weight from the tone on the word "high" in measure 17, in order to create the ethereal atmosphere demanded at this point.

—Practice vocalizing the canon, on a neutral vowel, found in measures 2–10 and 21–31, for a pure legato as well as to point up the composer's use of the canonic style.

—Note meter changes 3/4 to 2/4 to 4/4 found throughout the song, as an aid to memorization as well as an aid to interpretation.

—Use care in pronouncing "wonder," measures 24–25. Remember to maintain the stability of the vowel, only singing the "r" when ready to leave the word.

—Listen for pitch accuracy in measures 15–16, $c\#^2$–b^1–d^2.

Orpheus with his lute

William Shakespeare
(From "Henry VIII")

William Schuman

William Schuman

William Schuman, a composer who has carried on a remarkable dual career in music, was born in New York City on August 4, 1910. There was little in his family background to encourage development in the creation of serious music. He studied the violin in a haphazard manner and "picked up" various other instruments. The popular idiom was his first interest. During the high school years he had a jazz band and wrote popular songs as well as special material for club performers. His first publication was "In Love With You" to Frank Loesser's lyrics.

The turning point in Schuman's life came at the age of nineteen, when he first heard a symphony concert. This event provided the inspiration to begin serious study of music. Although he had enrolled in New York University's School of Commerce in preparation for a business career, he immediately withdrew and instead enrolled in the Malkin School of Music.

The year 1935 was an important one in the life of William Schuman. After returning from a summer at the Salzburg Mozarteum he began his first teaching position at Sarah Lawrence College, where he was to remain for ten years. Also, he began two years of study in composition with Roy Harris. Progress was rapid for the young composer, despite his late start. His "Second Symphony" was played by the Boston Symphony Orchestra under Koussevitzky in 1939. His "Third Symphony," performed by the Boston Symphony Orchestra in 1941, won the first award of the Critics Circle of New York in 1942. The cantata, "A Free Song," won the Pulitzer Prize in music in 1943. In 1939 and 1940 he held Guggenheim fellowships, and in 1943 he won the composition award of the American Academy of Arts and Letters. In 1949 the University of Wisconsin awarded him an honorary doctorate in music.

During his tenure as president of the Juilliard School, one of his outstanding contributions to music education was in the area of theoretical studies, with the creation of a new department called Literature and Materials of Music. In 1962 he resigned this position to become president of the Lincoln Center for the Performing Arts in New York City, where he remained until 1968.

Despite the heavy demands of administrative work, Schuman continued to produce a large body of works, including nine symphonies; four ballets; four string quartets, as well as other chamber works for various instruments; one opera; a piano concerto; a violin concerto; choral works; piano works; and songs.

William Schuman has left a definite stamp upon the life of American music through his wide-ranging activities as a teacher, an administrator in key positions, and a composer in almost all forms of music. He personally has expressed his sense of privilege in being a part of the life of the art of music in so many and such varied ways.

Stylistic Features

"Orpheus with his lute" was composed in 1944. The penetrating statement from Shakespeare's *Henry VIII,* expressing the power of music to calm the forces of nature as well as the restless spirit of man, is sensitively interpreted by the composer.

A strong unifying element is provided by the rhythmic ostinato established in the four-measure introduction and sustained throughout the song. Any suspicion of monotony is prevented by irregularity in phrase length, both in the accompaniment and in the vocal line. This unusual feature begins at measure 5, where the first phrase of the vocal line extends from measures 5–12, whereas the accompaniment phrase ends in measure 10. The ostinato continues in measures 11–15, where the vocal line begins its second phrase. Again, the melody extends to measure 20 whereas the accompaniment phrase ends in measure 18. This strategy of overlapping between the vocal line and the accompaniment continues throughout the entire song, providing added continuity.

The harmonic progression in the piano introduction (I–IV–V with a 4–3 suspension) is repeated many times throughout: measures 7–10, 11–14, 26–29, 36–39, the suspension on the dominant also appearing at 19–20, 24–25, 34–35, creating horizontal movement. The interesting change of meter that occurs at measures 10, 18, and 25 gives a sense of freedom of movement to the melodic line.

The modal melody of a limited range is written in an essentially scalewise manner. This aspect combined with the irregularities mentioned earlier provides a flowing, calm loveliness and a sense of continuity in keeping with the spiritual affirmation of the text. The modulation to D Major in measure 30 is especially positive in evoking the textual meanings of "In sweet music," and the return to the minor in measure 36 expressively responds to the word "die."

Specific Study Suggestions

The syllabic setting of this ode to music demands a smooth legato tonal line, clarity of diction, and a well-supported soft tone for an ideal interpretation.

—Discuss text meanings in relation to the Shakespeare play.
—Be reminded that the limited dynamic level, which must be carefully observed for expressive purposes, needs good tonal support.
—Carefully observe purity of vowel pronunciation throughout.
—Extrapolate measures 22–24, 29–31, 31–33 for vocalization on a neutral vowel, as an aid in solving the tessitura problems presented. As an interesting exercise, experiment with the transposition of these measures, beginning with a lower key and gradually going higher. Follow such exercises with the use of the text.
—Maintain height in the tone on the descending scale passages found in measures 10 and 25, making certain to avoid going into a pure chest tone.
—Observe meter changes 3/4 and 4/4 found throughout song, as an aid to memorization.

LULLABY OF THE LAKE

CONSUELO CLOOS   ALAN HOVHANESS

Alan Hovhaness

The conventional musical training of Alan Hovhaness, who was born in Somerville, Massachusetts, on March 8, 1911, gave little indication of the future direction of his work in composition. However, by the time he was thirty years old he had become irresistibly drawn to the art expression of the Middle East through the influence of colleagues at the Armenian Orthodox Church of St. James in Watertown, Massachusetts, where he was organist. The result of this spiritual kinship with an ancient culture was the decision to destroy his total creative output up to that time, consisting of some one thousand manuscripts, and to devote the remainder of his life to a linking of the cultures of the East and West in his music.

From this time on Hovhaness's compositional style was completely changed and totally different from that of any other American composer. He studied the musics of the Near East, the Middle East, and the Far East, as well as Eastern geography, backgrounds, culture, and people. He used the techniques of Western music to express the spirituality of the East and, conversely, has used Eastern musical techniques and instruments in his music.

Hovhaness has contributed a very large and distinguished repertoire of exotic and atmospheric works to the musical world. The catalogue of over two hundred works includes twenty-three symphonies; concertos for orchestra; chamber works in a wide variety of instrumental combinations; ballets; organ works; piano works; three one-act operas and one full-length opera; choral music; and songs. The composer has concerned himself with a search for the purest practicable musical sounds in order to achieve a sense of the serenity and peace of Eastern music. His aim has been to achieve a clear and tranquil effect by means of the repetition and ornamentation characteristic of Eastern music.

Alan Hovhaness has been honored with many distinguished awards for his creative work. The University of Rochester awarded him an honorary doctorate in 1958, and in 1959 Bates College made a similar award. In 1951 the National Institute of Arts and Letters awarded him a grant. In 1953 and 1955 he received Guggenheim fellowships. He received a Fulbright Fellowship for research in the music of India and Japan in 1959–60. In 1962 he received a Rockefeller Grant for research in the ancient court music of Japan and Korea, and in 1965 he engaged in a cultural exchange tour of Soviet Russia.

Stylistic Features

"Lullaby of the Lake," to a text by Consuelo Cloos, was composed in 1969. A two-voiced contrapuntal scheme is the unusual feature of this setting. The accompaniment theme is a sprightly dancelike melody, utilizing a hypnotic rhythmic pattern that provides a strong unifying element. In contrast, the flowing vocal line, limited to a six-note range, reflects the rhapsodic nature of the text.

The accompaniment, which is written in the dorian mode with brief excursions into the aeolian (measures 16, 23, 43), employs a single voice sounding above the vocal line. The modality as well as the placement of the accompaniment might be said to create an illusion of Middle Eastern atmospheric effects. The legato style of the vocal melody is in sharp contrast to the strongly rhythmic and lively piano accompaniment. However, they are completely complementary due to their iterative nature, the thin texture, and the common modality.

Specific Study Suggestions

"Lullaby of the Lake" is an unusually useful song for the study of legato and for the development of the capability of a rapid breath intake. The singer must capture the hypnotic and serene quality of the ceaseless melody linked to a mystical text by means of purity of tone, smoothness of line, and clarity of diction. In view of the fact that no dynamic indications have been made, it may be assumed that the composer intended the interpreter to sing with a mezzo-piano, flutelike tone. Such a tone would be entirely in keeping with the prevailing tranquility of the mood.

—Vocalize the melody on "OO," phrase by phrase, for the development of the legato needs.
—Apply the text with attention to the maintenance of resonant purity of tone.
—Maintain stability of the vowels for perfect intonation in the following instances: "air" in measures 22–23; "hair" in measures 28–30; "there" in measures 38–40.
—Careful planning for rapid breath inhalation is necessary as no rests are indicated in "Lullaby of the Lake." In each case the breath should be inconspicuous and in no way interrupt the tonal flow of the melismatic setting. The following breath indications are recommended:

- The end of measures 6 and 10
- After "grace" measure 14
- After "embrace" measure 18
- After "breath" measure 21
- Before "my" measure 24
- After "mist" measure 27
- Before "beloved" measure 34
- After "wilt" measure 37
- The end of measures 40 and 44
- After "dreaming" measure 46

—Note independent character of the vocal line, which indicates the necessity of studying it apart from the accompaniment.
—Keep in mind the importance of a well-supported, light, and flexible tone for the rapid tempo.
—Note the sequential treatment of the accompaniment, as an aid to memorization.

For Dorothy Boothe

Begone, Dull Care

High in A major   Low in F major

Tune and Words
ENGLISH TRADITIONAL
Set by
JOHN EDMUNDS

clay. _____ My wife shall sing and I shall dance And mer-ri- ly pass the
(spouse)

day, _____ For I hold it one of the wis - est things to drive dull care a -

way.

John Edmunds

John Edmunds, composer and musicologist, was born in San Francisco, California, on June 10, 1913. Early music study was at the Curtis Institute of Music in Philadelphia, where his principal teacher was Rosario Scalero. He earned his M.A. degree at Harvard University, where he studied composition under Walter Piston. Advanced study followed, first at Cornell University under Roy Harris and later at Columbia University under Otto Luening.

The art song, of which form he has composed over five hundred, has been the primary compositional interest of John Edmunds. In a letter to this author he states that "most of the texts are by W. B. Yeats or anonymous Middle English though in my earlier years I set a number of lyrics by A. E. Housman." Edmunds is also noted for his "realizations" of the works of Henry Purcell as well as for his settings of numerous folk songs. The composer has expressed his appreciation of the value and the beauty of folk songs, as well as the importance of the sense of continuity they provide from generation to generation. He has praised both the texts and the melodic material of the folk song; the texts as being reflective of the hidden emotional lives of all who speak English, not only that of a single poet, and the folk music as being the source for all music.

The composer's distinguished scholarly career has included service on the faculties of Columbia University and the University of California at Berkeley. From 1957 to 1961 he was in charge of the Americana Collection in the Music Division of the New York Public Library. Presently, John Edmunds is engaged in research on the English song from John Dowland to Henry Purcell.

Stylistic Features

"Begone Dull Care," an English folk song, was tastefully set by John Edmunds in 1953. Simple diatonic harmonies are employed in keeping with the unpretentious, cheerful text. The charming folk melody is of a limited range and is essentially scalewise in nature.

The musical interest of this lilting song is found in the imaginative use of extremely simple material. In the bass line of measure 9 an imitation of the melodic line of measure 3 is found. In the treble line of the accompaniment in measure 11 an imitation of the melodic line of measure 10 is heard. Ingenious variations of the canonic idea begin in the melody of measures 12–18, which is repeated with slight variation in the bass line of the accompaniment in measures 15–21. The treble of the accompaniment then uses the same melodic material as an interlude in measures 22–25.

In the second strophe the canon idea is altered. The melody found in measure 26 is immediately taken up in the treble line of the accompaniment in measure 27 and played an octave higher than the voice. This plan is extended throughout the second strophe and the material of the last measure of the melody is used to provide a charming and suitable postlude.

Specific Study Suggestions

"Begone Dull Care" should be sung with the joyous buoyancy suggested by the text. The scalewise vocal line and the limited range of the melody present few problems for the singer. However, since this song is essentially a syllabic setting, it is an ideal study in clear diction.

—Work for flexibility of the lips and tongue in the formation of the consonants; but at no time should there be any interference with the pronunciation of the vowels.

—Isolate selected passages such as measures 6–7, 10–11, 13–14, and 18 as an exercise in lip and tongue flexibility.

—Experiment with both a marcato and a legato style of singing in order to determine the most suitable for interpretive purposes.

—Notice slight melodic alterations between the first and second strophes as found in measures 6 and 28, 9 and 31, 13 and 34, 15 and 37, 16 and 38, 17 and 39.

—Discuss change in mood of the text between strophes one and two, and reflect these changes in the interpretation.

For Carl Hague and Gladys Steele

Billy Boy

AMERICAN SAILORS' CHANTY
Setting by JOHN EDMUNDS

charm-in' Bil-ly Boy.

Can she cook a bit of steak,

Bil-ly Boy, Bil-ly Boy? Can she cook a bit of steak, me Bil-ly

Boy? _____ She can cook a bit of steak,___ Ay,___ and

make a grid-dle cake, Han-sy dan-sy, kit-tle me fan-cy, O me

Stylistic Features

"Billy Boy," a vigorous American sailor's chanty, was imaginatively set by John Edmunds in 1953. The spirited, strophic melody is of limited range and is essentially scalewise in nature. By means of ingenious variations in the accompaniment from strophe to strophe, the composer provides relief from the repetitiveness of the melody. In the first strophe, block chords are utilized, which immediately establishes a strong feeling for the ongoing rhythm of the chanty. In the second strophe, essentially the same harmonization is used, but of a lighter texture. In the left hand a single pedal-type note is utilized, whereas in the right hand the chord is broken.

The third strophe starts out with a decided change of texture, a two-voice setting with the accompaniment providing a counter-melody. At measure 25, however, the texture becomes fuller again, and considerable chromaticism appears in measure 26. In the fourth strophe the composer reverts to a block chord type of setting. There is no postlude.

Specific Study Suggestions

"Billy Boy" should be sung forthrightly and vigorously, with a strong sense of the relentless rhythm. The humor of the story must be brought out in the interpretation by means of careful dynamic variation as well as by the use of extremely clear diction.

—At first, practice slowly, taking care that the melodic rhythm is precisely correct. Note the melodic syncopations, as in measures 3, 9, 12, 18, 21, 27, 31, 37.
—Choral-speak the text while conducting, in order to emphasize the importance of text clarity by means of flexibility of the tongue and lips.
—Take care to utilize dynamic variety from strophe to strophe. A class discussion of this problem would be appropriate.
—The antiphonal nature of the text provides an interesting opportunity for the class. The group may be divided, one asking the questions, the other providing the answers.

I'm Nobody

Emily Dickinson

Vincent Persichetti
Op. 77, No. 2

Vincent Persichetti

Vincent Persichetti was born in Philadelphia on June 6, 1915. In earliest childhood his exceptional musical gifts became evident and by the age of eleven years he was playing the piano professionally in local orchestras. At fifteen he was appointed organist and music director of St. Mark's Reformed Church in Philadelphia, and at seventeen he was appointed music director of the Arch Street Presbyterian Church in the same city, where he remained until 1946.

Persichetti attended the Combs College of Music in Philadelphia, graduating with the bachelor of music degree in 1936. The study of conducting followed, under Fritz Reiner at the Curtis Institute of Music. From 1939 to 1941 he was a scholarship student of Olga Samaroff Stokowski in piano and Paul Nordoff in composition at the Philadelphia Conservatory of Music. His summers during that period were spent studying composition with Roy Harris. A long and distinguished teaching career began in 1939 at Combs College, where he headed the composition department until 1942. In that year he moved to the Philadelphia Conservatory of Music to head its composition department, where he remained until 1962. In 1947 he began teaching composition at the Juilliard School of Music and subsequently headed the department.

Persichetti was first recognized as a gifted creative talent with the performance of his "Fables" for narrator and orchestra by the Philadelphia Symphony Orchestra under Eugene Ormandy in 1945, but it was with the performance of his Symphony No. 3 by the same orchestra in 1947 that he emerged as a major American composer. He has written major works in all the large forms except opera. His works include seven symphonies; thirteen serenades (suite-like compositions in free style for various combinations of instruments); piano works, including eleven piano sonatas; three string quartets and other chamber works for various instrumental combinations; choral works; and numerous songs.

Stylistic Features

"I'm Nobody," the second of four songs, Op. 77, to Emily Dickinson texts, was composed in 1958. The sprightly charm and good humor of the text is carried out in every aspect of this setting, a song in A Major (no key signature). The bright mood is established in the introduction by the use of strongly accented rhythms and syncopation. A momentary change of feeling occurs in measures 25–32. At this point the use of a sustained chordal accompaniment fluctuating between major and minor chords successfully dramatizes the drollery of "They'd banish us, you know." However, the brightness quickly returns with a variation of the initial accompaniment theme.

The melodic line of a limited range acquires an amusing and playful character in keeping with the textual meanings through its decisive rhythmic accentuations and ingenious syncopations. The entrance of the voice in measure 7 seems to be the completion of the introduction and effectively makes the statement "I'm Nobody." After this announcement the accompaniment reiterates the sprightly pattern of measures 1–2 before the question "Who are you?" Throughout the song each line of the text is effectively set off by the dancelike rhythmic figure noted in measure 1.

Specific Study Suggestions

The amusing rhythmic precision of the question-and-answer character between the melodic line and the accompaniment provides the singer with a clear guide to an effective interpretation of this charming and humorous song. Also, a sharp and crisp enunciation of the text is of importance in carrying out the composer's lighthearted intentions.

"I'm Nobody" is a most useful study in the problem of singing with a light tone and, at the same time, maintaining good support throughout. Further problems presented by this song are those of sustaining a tonal line while enunciating the text with the exaggerated clarity demanded by the mood, and negotiating the melodic leaps without interrupting the tonal line.

—Never allow the action of the lips, so necessary for clarity in enunciating consonants, to interfere with the tonal flow.

—In measures 12–13, maintain the stability of the vowels in negotiating the melodic leap from e^1 to b^1.

—Eliminate any suggestion of weight on the lower tone of the interval in measures 13–14.

—Exaggerate the vowel color in "you," measures 13–14, for interpretive effect.

—Listen for pitch on descending thirds in measures 7–8 and 23–24.

—Notice syncopated melodic rhythm as well as melodic and accompanimental suspensions in measures 20–22, which create humorous effect. Practice for precision.

—Experiment with vocal inflections for effective interpretation in measures 23–24, "don't tell"; measures 25–28, "they'd banish us"; measures 29–30, "how dreary."

—Practice the use of word accents found in measures 41–44 for interpretive purposes.

To Hildegarde Watson

DAVID MOURNS FOR ABSALOM

From The Second Book
of Samuel (18:33)

DAVID DIAMOND
(1946)

o - ver the gate, and there he

wept. _____ And as he went,

thus _____ he said: _____

"O _____ my son, _____ O my

God__ I had died for thee,_____ O

Ab - sa - lom, my son,_____ O__ Ab - sa -

lom,__ my__ son,_____ O_____ my__

son!"_____ lunga

*Press key down silently

July 26, 1946
Rochester, N.Y.
New York, N.Y.

David Diamond

David Diamond, born in Rochester, New York, on July 9, 1915, displayed his unusual creative gift as a child. In 1927 the family moved to Cleveland, where Andre de Ribaupierre, a faculty member of the Cleveland Institute of Music, befriended the youthful musician and provided the means for Diamond's earliest musical training. Returning to Rochester in 1930, Diamond continued his studies with Effie Knauss in violin and with Bernard Rogers in composition. Four years later as a scholarship winner at the New Music School in New York, he became the pupil of Paul Boepple in improvisation and of Roger Sessions in composition.

In 1937 Diamond joined the procession of young composers going to Paris to study with Nadia Boulanger. It was she who introduced him to Igor Stravinsky, who spent considerable time with Diamond in diagnosing the compositional problems in "Psalm for Orchestra," a work which was later partially responsible for the award of a Guggenheim scholarship. Numerous prizes and scholarships were to follow, which were not only important to his financial survival as a composer, but also provided important recognition of his work.

David Diamond has composed prolifically in many forms. The long list of his creations includes orchestral works, including nine symphonies; two violin concertos; a cello concerto and a piano concerto; chamber works, including two string quartets; sonatas for the cello and violin; vocal works including madrigals, choruses and more than one hundred songs. In his songwriting, Diamond has been attracted to texts that are widely diversified in expressive range and of a deep spiritual nature. He has spoken of his text selections in relation to his particular melodic, polyphonic, and harmonic style

as providing a natural continuation of the art song in the twentieth century.

Stylistic Features

"David Mourns for Absalom," an early song of the composer, was composed in 1946. The powerful Biblical text depicts the overwhelming grief of King David upon the death of his son, Absalom. The setting is powerful, in keeping with the nobility of this account of a father's expression of love for his rebellious son.

The solemn, modal melody of this through-composed song enables both the performer and the listener to go back in time and to participate in the historic tragedy. The melody is slow-moving throughout and is characterized by scalewise passages and small skips. At the climactic point in measure 48 the voice is taken into a higher register in keeping with the intensity of the text, "Would God I had died for thee." The expressive leap in measure 61 on "son" is notably powerful; thereafter, the melody immediately begins to subside in intensity, in keeping with the textual meaning.

The accompaniment throughout is characterized by heavy block chords descriptive of the weight of David's grief. The harmonies are largely diatonic, and dissonances are created by traditional means (suspensions, appoggiaturas, added seconds and ninths).

This song appears to present the unusual feature of a piece ending in a different key from its beginning key: F Major, ending in c minor. This carries out the textual meanings with good effect, when it can be seen that the section from measures 1–28, with the melody in the aeolian mode, is a narrative prelude, whereas the following material, starting at measure 29, is David's actual lament. This "aria" section, starting and ending in g minor, includes a brief but dramatic modulation to D Major, which coincides with the climax of the text "Would God I had died for thee."

Specific Study Suggestions

"David Mourns for Absalom" is an excellent study for the development of a full, dramatic, unforced tone in the middle and upper middle of the voice, in response to the inherent drama of the text.

—Sing the narrative prelude in measures 6–28 in a straightforward manner with a full and well-supported tone.

—In measures 27–28 a molto crescendo begins on d^2 on "said," leading into the cry "O my son" on e^{b2} in measure 29. The maximum tonal support necessary for such a strenuous and dramatic passage demands that the singer consciously involve maximum support of the lower abdominal muscles in resistance to the diaphragm.

—Study the aria section, measures 29–61, with a moderate tonal volume in order to avoid the possibility of vocal strain. Necessary drama for an effective interpretation may be added later.

—Sing the last phrase of the song, measures 67–71, with a sorrowful quietude in keeping with the father's final acceptance of his tragedy.

—Note meter change in measures 54–55 and its effect on the drama of the text.

—Note key changes adding to the dramatic effect: F Major, measures 1–28; c minor, measures 29–43; D Major, measures 44–45; c minor, measures 55–73.

—Carefully phrase melismatic setting of such words as "grieved" in measure 8; "Absalom" in measures 35–38, 39–40, and 62–66; "would God," measures 54–55.

—Note the "weeping" or "sigh" motive in melody of measures 62–65, characteristic of the Baroque era. Be aware of the importance of this phrase in depicting the release of tension following the climax of the song. Other "sigh" motives may be found in measures 35–40, 51–52.

—Carefully monitor the easy functioning of the jaw in the study of this song. Care in this respect is especially important for tonal beauty in forte singing.

To James and Mia Agee
This World Is Not My Home

Anonymous

DAVID DIAMOND
(1946)

Stylistic Features

"This World Is Not My Home," an early song of the composer, was written in 1946. The philosophical text speaks of the longing of the human spirit to go beyond the river of this life into the great sea of eternity. The setting is quiet and serene, in keeping with the spiritual acceptance of the inevitability of the text meanings.

The melody of this short, through-composed song is moderately slow-moving throughout and is characterized by small skips and scalewise passages. The dynamic range of the melody is limited. However, the interpreter is invited to provide greater tonal intensity in measures 10–12 in response to the textual needs. The left hand of the accompaniment provides a sense of calm motion throughout, which might be said to depict the river of life. The harmonies are diatonic, and dissonances are provided by traditional means, notably added seconds, ninths, etc., which give the primary chords an impressionistic effect.

Specific Study Suggestions

"This World Is Not My Home" provides an excellent opportunity for a study in legato singing. The text demands a quiet intensity in the interpretation, but the limited dynamic range precludes any temptation on the part of the young singer to "force" the tone.

—Vocalize each phrase on a neutral vowel before applying the text, as an aid to achieving a good legato tone.
—Be reminded to fully support the tone despite the limited dynamic needs.
—Note meter changes in measures 4, 9, 10, 12, 14, and 15 for their effect on the interpretation.
—Make certain that the melodic syncopation found in measures 7–8 is sung with the rhythmic precision important for a good interpretation.
—Take care that the text is clearly enunciated throughout, without disturbing the legato needs.

To Mrs. Lawrence Gilman

STOPPING BY WOODS ON A SNOWY EVENING

ROBERT FROST   JOHN LA MONTAINE

John La Montaine

Pulitzer Prize–winning composer John La Montaine was born in Oak Park, Illinois, in 1920. He studied at the Eastman School of Music, graduating with the B.M. degree in 1942. His principal teachers at the Eastman School were Bernard Rogers and Howard Hanson. Elsewhere, he studied with Stella Roberts, Bernard Wagenaar, and Nadia Boulanger. A pianist of virtuoso caliber, La Montaine was pianist and celestist with the NBC Symphony Orchestra under Arturo Toscanini from 1950 to 1954.

Renown came to La Montaine with the awarding of the Pulitzer Prize in 1959 for his "Concerto for Piano and Orchestra," Op. 9. Commissions and awards followed this initial prize and included two Guggenheim fellowships as well as commissions from the Ford Foundation and the Koussevitzky Foundation. Also, the composer was awarded the Rheta Sosland Chamber Music Competition prize in 1961 for his "String Quartet," Op. 16. He has served as composer-in-residence at the American Academy in Rome and has been a visiting professor of composition at various universities including his alma mater, the Eastman School of Music.

A concern for the discovery of new sources of creative inspiration beyond the technical tools available to composers has led La Montaine to an extensive investigation of the sounds of nature. He has expressed the belief that the art of music has lost sight of its base in the natural world and, in the process, has become overly refined and in danger of decay. It is his conviction that the natural sounds of animals and birds can provide the richest possible source of raw material for the creator of music and bring a new vitality to the art.

La Montaine has composed in many forms. His interest in the sounds of nature is responsible for a series of works including "Birds of Paradise," Op. 34, for piano and orchestra; "Missa Naturae," Op. 37, for chorus, narrator and orchestra; and "Wilderness Journal," Op. 41, a symphony for bass-baritone, organ and orchestra. He has composed three operas to form a "Christmas Trilogy": "Novellis, Novellis," Op. 31; "The Shepherds Playe," Op. 38; and "Erode the Greate," Op. 40. Also, the composer has written numerous choral works, chamber works, piano and organ works, and songs.

Stylistic Features

"Stopping by Woods on a Snowy Evening," to a text by Robert Frost, was published in 1963. The delightful text of the traveler ruminating on the beauties of the woods filling up with snow is set with quiet simplicity in keeping with this mood. In the short introduction a pedal tone or drone on the tonic begins in the accompaniment and is maintained throughout the first section of the ternary setting. A charming pictorial effect of the slowly but steadily moving sleigh is thus created. The use of the neighboring C# with D in the accompanying treble part of the A section of the song illustrates an occasional jingling of the sleigh bell. This effect is further enhanced by the suggestion of the dominant in fifths and fourths in the treble of the accompaniment beginning with measure 7 and transferred to a higher register beginning in measure 8. This idea of a spare-textured and widely spaced harmonic overlay lends enchantment to the beauty of the moment.

Of special interest in a consideration of the melody is the careful dislocation of the poetic rhythms in the setting. These frequently occurring syncopations can be found in almost every measure and provide an expressive folklike touch and rhythmic variety to the song.

At section B in measure 16 the F Major chord points up the text. The B♭ in measure 21 darkens the word "frozen" in an expressive, pictorial manner. Also, the fluctuation in the meter in measures 19 and 22–24 enables the composer to treat the text with greater freedom. In preparation for the return to the A² section the g pedal is reintroduced in measure 24, and again the bell-like quality of the neighboring C#–D is heard as the little horse "gives his harness bells a shake."

The salient point of the song is reached in measure 38, where the composer augments the rhythmic pattern and gives it a pianissimo dynamic marking to emphasize the poetic thought. This momentary introspection ends with a C Major chord in measure 44, with an inkling of a g minor in the melody. Again, the pedal on G is heard in measure 45 and the song ends with the sound of the sleigh bell.

Specific Study Suggestions

A consideration of the reflective text is of first importance for the performer of "Stopping by Woods on a Snowy Evening." If the singer is able to imagine the quiet enjoyment of a sleigh ride in deserted woods "filling up with snow" and to sense the peace and wonder of the sight, he will reflect this mood in every aspect of his mien.

This song offers an interesting study in melodic rhythm. The syncopations found throughout the melodic line must be sung effortlessly and without dynamic stress, not only to maintain the quietude of the introspective mood but also to project the monotony of the moving sleigh.

—Rhythmically speak the text and, at the same time, gently conduct in order to develop rhythmic precision.
—Give particular attention to measures 4, 6, 7, 9, and 10, as the syncopated patterns found in these are typical of those found throughout the song. As rhythmic mastery is gained, the singer will find that he is able to sing the graceful melodic line with the simplicity and gentleness demanded by the text meanings.
—Take care to avoid overweighting the d¹ in the octave interval found in measures 2–4 and reiterated repeatedly throughout the song. Should weight be placed on the d¹, the line could be distorted and so adversely affect the ruminative coloration.
—Have a sense of "singing through the rests" as a furtherance of the atmospheric quality of the moving sleigh.
—Listen for pitch accuracy in skips of the fifth, as found in measures 12 and 32.
—Listen for pitch accuracy on accidentals found in measures 21–22, 40, 42–43.
—Carefully note meter changes throughout as an aid in memorization.
—Note tempo changes in measures 16–25 and 39–43 as important for expressive purposes.
—Do not permit the syncopation in the accompaniment figuration, which creates a polyrhythmic effect between the melody and accompaniment, to interrupt the melodic flow.

Sing Agreeably Of Love

W. H. Auden   Daniel Pinkham

gree - a - bly, a - gree - a - bly, a - gree - a - bly — of
gree - a - bly, a - gree - a - bly, a - gree - a - bly — of

love, — love, — love, — love, — a - gree - a - bly of —

love. —

(v^{ts} 2) Put a gold ring on her fin - ger, And press — her close to your

Daniel Pinkham

Daniel Pinkham, who was to build an important career as a composer, keyboard artist, and conductor, was born in Lynn, Massachusetts, on June 5, 1923. He took both his B.A. and M.A. degrees at Harvard University, where he studied with A. Tillman Merritt, Walter Piston, and Archibald T. Davison. Later he studied with Samuel Barber, Arthur Honegger, and Nadia Boulanger at Tanglewood. He studied harpsichord with Putnam Aldrich and Wanda Landowska, and organ with E. Power Biggs.

Pinkham's wide-ranging musical interests have included teaching and conducting as well as composing. He has been a member of the faculty of the New England Conservatory of Music since 1959 and musical director of King's Chapel, Boston, since 1958. Other posts have included brief periods at Simmons College, Boston University, and Harvard University.

The large catalogue of Daniel Pinkham's compositions includes works in many forms: opera and symphony, chamber works, concerti for various instruments, organ works, choral works including cantatas, motets and madrigals, and songs. His interest in electronic music has led him to compose works for tape alone, as well as many with tape and chorus, solo instruments, and ensembles. Other forms have included organ with instruments, chorus with instruments, voice with instruments, theatre works, and film and TV music.

Pinkham's music has been characterized by Roger Scanlan as concise in form with a high degree of craftsmanship and noted for its accessibility to the listener. The songs, although limited in number, cover a wide-ranging gamut of emotion and are noted for their charm and distinction.

Stylistic Features

"Sing Agreeably of Love," to a text by W. H. Auden, was published in 1949. The folklike melody is characterized by a repetitive modal quality of limited range as well as the dotted rhythmic pattern in six-eight.

The musical interest of this unusual song is to be found in the piano accompaniment. A pedal-like figure introduced in the short, four-measure introduction is carried out elsewhere in the song. Beginning in measure 13 the composer utilizes great variation in the accompanimental rhythmic structure to effectively underline the repetitiveness of the text "Sing agreeably of love." The use of peripheral chromatic triads at measures 16–18, repeated at 35–36 and 44–45, each time just before a return to "the beginning," lends charm and interest, as does also the final cadence with the picardy third.

The piano interlude in measures 20–24 reiterates the pedal of the introduction, and this idea is carried out through measure 27, where the accompaniment figure is enriched texturally by a greater fullness in the chordal structure. It might be suggested that this device could be in response to the cynicism evidenced in the text meanings at this point. Unexpected interest is found in the fact that no dominant harmony is used at any point, which helps to give the whole song its modal flavor.

Specific Study Suggestions

No hint of emotionalism should be evidenced in the interpretation of this sophisticated song. Rather, a light and lyric tone quality should prevail, in response to the composer's indication that it be sung in an easy, folklike manner.

—Be reminded of the importance of rhythmic precision.

—As an aid in the attainment of pitch accuracy, vocalize the melody on a neutral vowel before using the text in selected phrases.

—Memorize the melodic line apart from the accompaniment in order to assure melodic accuracy when singing with the unusual accompaniment.

—Practice with care such passages as in measures 8–11, 15–17, etc. listening for pitch accuracy.

—Enunciate text clearly in order to "tell the story."

—Take care to color the voice imaginatively in singing the repetitive texts found in such passages as measures 12–20 and 31–52.

to Pierre Quézel

Early in the Morning

ROBERT HILLYER   NED ROREM

Ned Rorem

Ned Rorem was born in Richmond, Indiana, on October 23, 1923. His earliest study of composition was under Max Wald in Chicago. After attending Northwestern University for two years, 1940–42, he won a scholarship to the Curtis Institute of Music, where he graduated in 1947. From Curtis he went to the Juilliard School of Music to study composition with Bernard Wagenaar; there, he was awarded the M.M. degree in 1948 and the M.S. degree in 1949. During the summer of 1947 he studied at the Berkshire Music Center at Tanglewood with Aaron Copland. Also during this period, he studied with Virgil Thomson.

Several important prizes—the Gershwin Memorial Award in 1943, the Lili Boulanger Award in 1950, and a Fulbright Fellowship in 1951—enabled Rorem to live and study in Paris until 1955. In 1957 he was awarded a Guggenheim Fellowship.

Ned Rorem's compositional output has been prodigious. Not only has he written more than three hundred songs but he has also composed operas, chamber works, string works, symphonies, choral works, ballets, piano works, theatre works, and incidental music. Recognition has come to the composer not only in the form of awards, but also in important performances. His opera *Miss Julie,* which was funded by the Ford Foundation, was performed by the New York City Center Opera in 1965. Noted conductors who have programmed his works have included Leonard Bernstein, Eugene Ormandy, Leopold Stokowski, Dimitri Mitropoulis, Paul Paray, Alfred Wallenstein, and Fritz Reiner.

Serious consideration must be given the songs of Rorem, if for no other reason than his uncommon attention to the song form and the proliferation of songs in his total creative output. In a study of the composer's songs as compared to the songs of twelve other distinguished song composers of the twentieth century, William North has found that Rorem gives his greatest attention to a flowing, arched melodic curve. The accompaniments, for the most part, mirror the text requirements and his harmonies display a preference for modality. The rhythms tend to be even and held within regular metres.

Rorem's concern for text considerations must also be pointed out. In an article published in 1959, the composer discussed at length the expressive power of text in evoking the musical mood.

Stylistic Features

"Early in the Morning," to a Robert Hillyer text, was composed in 1958. The ingenuous sing-song nature of the poem, depicting the musings of the young lover while sitting at the outdoor café in the early morning is expressed in faithful detail by the composer. Every phrase is exactly four measures in length except for the two-measure interlude (or extension) at measures 21–22. The vocal line itself utilizes but two different melodic phrases. The first appears in measures 5–8 and is repeated in measures 9–12. The second melodic phrase appears in measures 13–16 and is repeated in measures 17–20. The B section of this song in ternary form is a repetition of the earlier material a third higher (at measure 23). The return to the original key of B♭ at measure 39 indicates the return to the A section of the song. Further recurrences may be discerned in the bass line, being the same for measures 1–4, 4–8, 23–26 (in respective keys).

The accompaniment is of a light and transparent texture reminiscent of the style of the sophisticated café pianist. This aspect also strongly evokes the poetic setting of the café on the Rue François Premier.

Specific Study Suggestions

The pictorial effectiveness of the Hillyer text in evoking the pleasant mood of summertime in Paris clearly indicates to the performer of "Early in the Morning" the stylistic claims of the song. The translucent texture of the accompaniment, the simplicity of the vocal line, and the moderate dynamic levels found throughout distinctly point up the composer's intentions for its realization.

This song offers an opportunity to "tell a story" and to create a charming mood without encountering inordinate vocal difficulty. The melodic line is limited in range and, to a great extent, is scalewise in character. Also, the moderate tempo enables the performer to take the necessary time for the careful consideration of technical needs.

—The legato tonal line should be carefully supported despite the moderate dynamic levels found throughout the song.

—Clearly enunciate the text, without any jaw constriction.

—In measures 26–27, the leap from f^1 to d^{b2} demands careful attention to the modification of the vowel in the word "smell" toward AYE, as an aid to pitch accuracy.

—Strive for the attainment of good French diction for "Rue François Premier," "croissant" and "café au lait."

—Practice with the metronome for the establishment of the tempo indication and for insight into the importance of accurate tempo in establishing the nostalgic mood.

—Observe dynamic markings throughout for careful recreation of the rich poetic mood, which conveys visual as well as aural images.

Selected Sources for Additional Reading

Part I

Christy, Van A. *Expressive Singing*. Vol 2. 2d ed. Dubuque, Iowa: Wm. C. Brown Company Publishers, 1975.

Jacques, Reginald. *Voice Training in Schools*. London: Oxford University Press, 1953.

Rosewall, Richard B. *Handbook of Singing*. Evanston, Illinois: Summy-Birchard Company, 1961.

Part II

Kelsey, Franklin. *The Foundation of Singing*. London: William & Norgate, 1950.

Lehmann, Lilli. *How to Sing*. Translated by Richard Aldrich. New York: The Macmillan Company, 1905.

Vennard, William. *Singing, the Mechanism and the Technic*. Rev. ed., enl. New York: Carl Fischer, Inc., 1967.

Part III

Apel, Paul H. *Music of the Americas, North and South*. New York: Vantage Press, 1958.

Austin, William W. *Music in the 20th Century: from Debussy through Stravinsky*. New York: W. W. Norton & Company, Inc., 1966.

Bacon, Ernst. "Toward a Musical Home-Rule." *Bulletin of the American Composers Alliance* 7 (1958): 13–16.

Barbour, J. Murray. *The Church Music of William Billings*. East Lansing, Michigan: Michigan State University Press, 1960.

Briggs, John. *Leonard Bernstein*. Cleveland: World Publishing Company, 1961.

Broder, Nathan. *Samuel Barber*. New York: G. Schirmer, Inc., 1954.

Chase, Gilbert. *America's Music: From the Pilgrims to the Present*. Rev. 2d 3d. New York: McGraw-Hill Book Company, Inc., 1966.

Copland, Aaron. *The New Music, 1900–1960*. Rev. enl. ed. New York: W. W. Norton & Company, Inc., 1968.

Cowell, Henry, and Sydney Cowell. *Charles Ives and His Music*. New York: Oxford University Press, 1969.

Deri, Otto. *Exploring Twentieth Century Music*. New York: Holt, Rinehart and Winston, Inc., 1968.

Engel, Carl. *Music from the Days of George Washington*. Washington, D.C.: United States George Washington Bicentennial Commission, 1932.

Evett, Robert. "The Harmonic Idiom of Roy Harris." *Modern Music* 23 (Spring, 1946): 15–30.

Ewen, David. *Composers Since 1900: A Biographical and Critical Guide*. New York: H. W. Wilson Company, 1969.

Farwell, Arthur. "Pioneering for American Music." *Modern Music* 12 (Fall, 1924): 116–122.

Friedberg, Ruth C. *American Art Song and American Poetry.* 3 vols. Metuchen, N.J. and London: The Scarecrow Press, Inc., 1981, 1984, 1987.

Lowens, Irving. *Music and Musicians in Early America.* New York: W. W. Norton & Company, Inc., 1964.

Maisel, Edward M. *Charles T. Griffes.* New York: Alfred A. Knopf, 1943.

Marrocco, William T., and Harold Gleason. *Music in America.* New York: W. W. Norton & Company, Inc., 1964.

Mellers, Wilfrid. *Music in a New Found Land.* New York: Alfred A. Knopf, Inc., 1967.

Mornewek, Evelyn Foster. *Chronicles of Stephen Foster's Family.* 2 vols. Pittsburgh: University of Pittsburgh Press, 1944.

North, William Sills Wright. "Ned Rorem as a Twentieth Century Song Composer." D.M.A. dissertation. The University of Illinois, 1965. (Xerox copy. Ann Arbor: University Microfilms.)

Persichetti, Vincent, and Flora Rheta Schreiber. *William Schuman.* New York: G. Schirmer, Inc., 1954.

Reis, Claire. *Composers in America.* New York: The Macmillan Company, 1947.

Sablosky, Irving. *American Music.* Chicago: University of Chicago Press, 1969.

Salzman, Eric. *Twentieth Century Music: An Introduction.* Englewood Cliffs, New Jersey: Prentice-Hall, Inc., 1967.

Scanlan, Roger. "Spotlight on American Composers—Daniel Pinkham." *National Association Teachers of Singing Journal* 33:2 (December, 1976): 36–37.

Schwartz, Elliott, and Barney Childs, eds. *Contemporary Composers on Contemporary Music.* New York: Holt, Rinehart & Winston, 1967.

Smith, Julia. *Aaron Copland.* New York: E. P. Dutton & Company, Inc., 1955.

Sonneck, Oscar G. T. *Early Concert Life in America (1731–1800).* Leipzig: Breitkopf & Hartel. 1907.

———. *Francis Hopkinson and James Lyon.* Washington, D.C.: By the Author, 1905

Southern, Eileen. *The Music of Black Americans: A History.* New York: W. W. Norton & Company, Inc., 1971.

Stevens, Denis, ed. *A History of the Art Song.* New York: W. W. Norton & Company, Inc., 1960.

Tangeman, Robert. "The Songs of Theodore Chanler." *Modern Music* 22 (May–June 1945): 227–233.

Upton, William Treat. *Art Song in America.* Boston: Oliver Ditson Company, 1930.

Index